Theology and Culture

Cascade Companions

The Christian theological tradition provides an embarrassment of riches: from scripture to modern scholarship, we are blessed with a vast and complex theological inheritance. And yet this feast of traditional riches is too frequently inaccessible to the general reader.

The Cascade Companions series addresses the challenge by publishing books that combine academic rigor with broad appeal and readability. They aim to introduce nonspecialist readers to that vital storehouse of authors, documents, themes, histories, arguments, and movements that comprise this heritage with brief yet compelling volumes.

Volumes in this Series:

Forthcoming Volumes:

Theology and Culture

A Guide to the Discussion

D. STEPHEN LONG

 CASCADE *Books* · Eugene, Oregon

THEOLOGY AND CULTURE
A Guide to the Discussion

Cascade Companions

Cascade Books
A Division of Wipf and Stock Publishers
199 W. 8th Ave., Suite 3
Eugene, OR 97401

ISBN 13: 978-1-55635-052-8

Cataloging-in-Publication data:

Theology and culture : a guide to the discussion / D. Stephen Long.

    x + 114 p.; 23 cm.

    Cascade Companions

    ISBN 13: 978-1-55635-052-8

    1. Christianity and culture. 2. Theology. I. Title II. Series

BR115 C8 L58 2008

Manufactured in the U.S.A.

Contents

Introduction

The importance of "culture" for theology has been a preoccupation from the late nineteenth to the twenty-first centuries. What follows is a guide to this discussion. It is not intended as an exhaustive analysis nor a definitive statement of this preoccupation. No single book could possibly achieve this, let alone a little guide such as this one. My hope is that interested readers might use this guide to begin a fuller study on this important preoccupation. This guide is intended to introduce readers into why this conversation matters and why, for better or worse, it will continue to do so. I think this preoccupation has a great deal to do with the conflicts, tensions, and stresses in the life of the contemporary church. Thus a good understanding of it could go a long way in helping us work through some of these conflicts, tensions, and stresses. Many of the impasses we face result from our inherited answers to the question how we should relate theology and culture. Often those inherited answers are repackaged under new names and called "new and improved." Some critical examination of them might move us beyond many of our well-worn theological debates. What follows then is a guide to the discussion, but it is by no means intended to be neutral or objective. It seeks to chart a direction (or directions) that might move us through this preoccupation with culture while retaining what is so essential to it. Although it is neither neutral nor objective, I do hope it is generous and liberal toward those with whom it will be clear I differ. Above all, of course, I hope it is true.

The discussion begins with lesson 1 by quickly noting the promises and perils of the modern preoccupation with the relationship between theology and culture. The promise is that we can and must speak about God within our cultural context. Of course, that is also inevitable. No one could possibly speak about God otherwise, which raises the question why we moderns think this claim that we must speak about God without our cultural context is either controversial or revelatory. It is a truism such as we must move our legs in order to walk from one place to the next. The peril is that we will begin to think and act as if our speaking of God only has to do with our cultural context, as if we cannot speak about the same God in different languages, times and cultures and recognize it is the same God.

The next four lessons, lessons 2–5, offer a very quick overview of the meaning and uses of the term culture. We begin by asking the basic question in lesson 2, "What is culture?" Nearly everyone uses the term, and everyone seems to have "culture," but when we try to explain what we mean by culture and how we use it, we run up against difficulties. Culture was once defined over and against "nature," but that term has become as complex and contested as culture. As noted in lesson 3, those two terms are increasingly confused. The confusion arises, in part, from the recognition of the importance of language in modern philosophy. Even if you the reader never had a course in philosophy, or never heard of the phrase, "the linguistic turn," this philosophical moment has most likely affected your life in some way. If you attend church, it most certainly has affected your life for it is one of the main reasons we have been preoccupied with the question of how to relate theology and culture. Lesson 4 examines language. It does so in order to arrive in lesson 5 at some recognition of the diverse ways in which we use the term culture. Only at this point can we enter into the discussion that matters most—"culture and God," which is the theme of the midpoint of the guide in lesson 6. We will of course address this theme throughout every lesson. It is what matters most. However, lesson 6 raises questions as to how we can speak of God, and how we can do so with any good conscience, when we realize that so many different cultures speak of God in diverse languages. These questions then get addressed by examining a number of important theological responses. Those responses are divided into two sets. The first set, lessons 7–9, examine some distinctly modern responses. The second set, lessons 11 and 12, examine some postmodern responses. In between these two sets of responses is lesson 10, a discussion of the importance of the cultures of modernity and postmodernity. What might we mean when we use those terms? This guide seeks to chart where we have been so that we might have some sense as to where we are going. Having been raised on a river I have always been fond of a metaphor used by Gerhard Lohfink. Theology is like rowing a boat. You can only move forward when you are looking backwards. The difficulty is that when the river is swift you may not wind up where you would like to be. This guide seeks to land us safely on the other side by thinking about where we have been. The currents of modern/postmodern culture are so rapid that I do not know if the guide points in the right direction. For that reason, it is at most an invitation to an ongoing discussion. Why has contemporary theology and the church been so preoccupied with the question of culture? Should we continue that preoccupation or move through it to something more, such as the question of truth? If or when we do so (it is inevitable), how might we maintain what we rightly learned from this preoccupation?

1

Theology and Culture:
the Promises and Perils

What has culture to do with theology and why even ask this question in the first place? Theology alone is a sufficiently difficult subject. Why make it more difficult by correlating it with something as difficult to explain as culture? Theology bears enough problems of its own; after all it is a science of God who is infinite, inexhaustible, and perfect. How does one explain such a being as God? How can this be a "science," a form of knowledge when God is not an object in the world that we can point to and say "this is it" or "here it is, just look at this." We cannot treat God as an object where we give a definition and categorize it like we would in a biology class. God cannot be placed within the normal classification system of kingdom, phylum, order, genus, and species. In fact, ancient Christian theologians expressly forbade thinking or speaking of God in these terms. They said "God cannot be placed within any category" using a famous Latin expression, *Deus non est genere.*

This simple expression entails a radical idea: God cannot be placed within any category larger than God in order

1

to understand God. If we can define God in a category that is more encompassing than what we mean by "God," then that larger category would truly be what we mean by "God" and our use of the term "God" would be subordinate to that larger category. This is why theology begins with the claim that God is not in a genus or that God is not in a category. We know this only because of the revelation given to Moses when God tells him that God's proper name is "I am." God alone is the one who truly is; God cannot be contained within any conceptual framework that we devise ourselves, even though we must use our conceptual systems in order to speak of God. This important theological idea is drawn from the first three commandments God gave to Moses:

1. "You shall have no other gods before me."

2. "You shall not make for yourself an idol, whether in the form of anything that is in heaven above or that is on the earth beneath, or that is in the water under the earth."

3. "You shall not make wrongful use of the name of the Lord your God, for the Lord will not acquit anyone who misuses his name" (Exodus 20:1–7 NRSV).

These commandments set the parameters for our speaking and writing of God, which is what theology is. We must speak about God in such a way that we do not, explicitly or implicitly, assume something greater, more perfect, more holy than God; for if we do then we will have set other gods before God. We will have fashioned for ourselves an idol. And finally we will have taken God's name in vain, that is to say we will have used it not in order to worship and glorify God, but to worship and glorify something other than God, which could only be something created and thus our worship and adoration will be empty—vain.

Given that these first three commandments set the parameters within which we must speak about God, doing theology is itself an awesome task. How can we speak or write about God without reducing the majesty of the Most Holy One to our conceptuality? This problem tempts some to what is called a "negative" or "apophatic" theology. "Apophatic" means the negation of what appears. Thus this negative or apophatic theology only tells us what cannot be said about God. All it can say is "God is not . . . ." While this is an important and essential element of theology, worship requires that we also say something positive about God, which is called "kataphatic" theology. We cannot simply be silent for God has commanded us to speak, preach, teach, worship, and adore; all of which requires that we use language to address God. If we do not use our language to express the object of our thought, speech, worship, and adoration, who is the Living God, then we will fail to keep the commandments. We must worship and love God above all else, and that requires that we creatures use our language, actions, habits, gestures, thoughts, etc. for love, worship, and adoration. This is why we must finally bring together "theology" and "culture." For as I shall argue below, our cultivation of language, action, habits, gestures, thoughts, etc. for specific purposes is what we mean when we use the term "culture."

When we speak about God, we do not use some private language that God gives us. We use everyday language; the language that allows us to communicate the most mundane things as well as the most sublime. For this reason, theology cannot be done without culture; that is both its promise and its peril. The promise is this:

- As God spoke to Moses and disclosed to him God's Name through communicative acts creatures can know and recognize, and as God spoke in and through Jesus giving the world God's presence, so we have the promise that in and through our creaturely means of communication, we too can speak about God and in so doing make the truth of God present in the world. This happens through a variety of means:

  a. The reading and preaching of the Word becomes God's Word.

  b. The gathered community becomes the Body of Christ.

  c. The bread and wine become the real presence of Christ.

  d. The Virgin's Womb becomes God's birthplace.

  e. The teaching of the church attains to true knowledge of the Unknown God.

This promise also contains perils:

- We imagine that our creaturely means of communication can contain God such that our use of the term "God" becomes nothing more than a projection of our own culture. This happens when:

  a. God's Word is considered to be nothing more than the reading and preaching of human words.

b. The gathered community imagines itself to have absorbed Christ's body into itself without remainder. The Risen Body of Christ is no longer needed because we imagine that we as a gathered community are all that is meant by Christ's body.

c. The sacrament becomes an object containing God like a jeannie in a bottle.

d. Human culture thinks it alone gives birth to the concept "God."

e. On the one hand, the Christian life is reduced to a correct formulation of propositions, as if knowing the right formulas is all that salvation entails. On the other hand, the church's teachings are viewed as nothing but decisions made by arbitrary political power, which can always be changed by some other act of political power.

These are the promises and perils that bringing theology and culture together holds forth. The promises and the perils are closely related. What is a promise can be a source of peril, and what appears perilous gives rise to the promise. We cannot always determine if what we are doing participates in the promise or the peril. But if we are to do theology, we must venture forth boldly, recognizing both the promises and perils every time we speak of God. This helps us answer the question why we should relate theology and culture. The answer is simple: we have no choice. Theology can only be done in cultural form. Using language is an essential aspect of what we mean by "culture." Theology is using language to speak about God.

We are commanded to do this, and we must believe it can be done or we would never say, "Thus says the Lord," "The Lord be with you," "This is the Word of the Lord," "The body of Christ broken for you," etc. That we can speak about God is the promise. But given that it will always be *some* culture's language that is spoken, it is also the peril.

Questions for Reflection

1. What is theology?
2. Why can God not be placed in a category?
3. What are some categories in which we might be tempted to place God?
4. If God cannot be placed in a category, how are we to speak of God?
5. Why can we not be content with a purely 'negative' theology, which only says what we cannot say about God without telling us anything positive about God?
6. What are the promises involved in bringing theology and culture together?
7. What are the perils in the correlation between theology and culture?

2

What Is Culture?

How can we speak about God without assuming that God is nothing but our speaking, nothing but our culture's effort to name what cannot be named? To answer this question we need to pay close attention to what we mean by culture, and how we use this very complex term both in our everyday language and especially in the language of faith. Defining either theology or culture is difficult, and any definition will be inadequate and contested. In fact, Raymond Williams, a pioneer in the sociology of culture, stated, "culture is one of the two or three most complicated words in the English language." Its complexity, he argued, is not only found in its "intricate historical development," which includes a shift from culture as a "noun of process" to a "metaphor" of human development, but also because "culture" has become a significant concept in "distinct and incompatible systems of thought."[1] Any discussion of culture must attend to these two concerns:

> *First*, culture is a metaphor and thus its precise meaning is difficult to discern. *Second*, as a metaphor, culture does not have the same significance

1. Williams, *Keywords*, 87.

among different disciplines. Nor does it mean only
one thing within them. Its meaning is in its use.

We will examine each of these concerns in turn.

Culture as Metaphor

Culture was once a noun similar in meaning to "cultivation."
It was the activity and final product of what farmers, gardeners and others did to nature. Early generations could literally
point to a "culture" by pointing to a strawberry patch or a
field of corn and say "that is what culture means; it is the
process that results in that." We still use the term culture in a
similar way in biological experiments and medical science. We
can point to the material growing in a petri dish and call it a
"culture." Such a use of the term "culture" is not metaphorical;
it is literal. Culture names the thing growing in the petri dish.
But over the years the term "culture" shifted from a noun of a
process to a "metaphor." This occurred when culture no longer applied to a discussion of what people did to the soil and
other "natural" phenomena and instead applied the term to
what happens to people. When this occurred, culture became
a metaphor.

What does it mean to argue, as Williams does, that culture shifted from a noun of process to a metaphor? It means
that today we often think of "culture" not as the process and
product of what people do to "nature," which results in strawberries and growths in petri dish, but what happens to people
themselves. Culture is a metaphor for a kind of "cultivation"
that occurs to people through their practices, language, communities, doctrines, etc. Where "culture" once meant how
one tilled the soil; today it has more to do with how persons

themselves are "tilled." And that is why culture is such a difficult term. I can easily point to a farmer riding on his "cultivator" (an old-style farm implement that would cover weeds by churning up the soil over them) and know what is meant by the term "cultivator," but what culture means when I use it as a metaphor for a process that happens to people is much more difficult to discern.

To understand culture as a metaphor for human cultivation, we must first answer the question, what is a metaphor? A metaphor is a surprising conjunction of terms. For instance if I say "God has the whole world in his hands," I am using the metaphor "God's hands." I do not literally mean God has hands even though I do literally mean God has everything in God's hands. If someone asks me, "How many hands does God have?", then they failed to understand how I am using language. I would respond by saying, "I didn't mean for you to take it literally, it was a metaphor."

Metaphors are notoriously difficult to explain. I can give a definition for each of the words in the expression, "God has the whole world in his hands," but would such definitions really lead to fuller understanding? They could be misleading. This is not because we would mistake the literal for the metaphorical reading; for if we do not understand the literal meaning of "God," "has," "whole," "world," and "hands," the metaphor cannot work. The philosopher Donald Davidson has argued "metaphors mean what the words in their most literal interpretation mean, and nothing more." We cannot substitute some alternative "true" meaning of the words in a metaphor for the literal meaning in order to understand it. A metaphor is literal. But as Davidson also argues, "metaphor belongs exclusively to the domain of use."[2]

To make sense of a metaphor, we must know its literal meaning. Metaphorical meaning is not some alternative kind of meaning to the literal meaning, as if we somehow always translate the literal words into some other kind of words. Yet we cannot fixate on the literal meaning and think the metaphor seeks a one-to-one correspondence between the words used and that to which they refer. The metaphor used above would not work if someone began a search for God's hands. Instead, as Davidson notes, metaphors "make us attend to some likeness, often a novel or surprising likeness, between two or more things."[3] How does this help us understand culture? The term "culture" is a metaphor that posits a surprising likeness between a process that once applied to working the earth, which we now apply to human beings. We understand it best when we do not seek some "figurative" or "metaphorical" meaning but read it as a literal term now used metaphorically. For instance, if we do not know the literal meaning of the term "culture," we will fail to see its interesting use as a "metaphor" for human cultivation. We will forget that it is a surprising conjunction of terms. Therefore, rather than beginning with a succinct definition of the term "culture," I think more headway will be gained in understanding if we look less to the definition of the term "culture." in order to understand it and more to how we use it.

Let me give an example of how this works. Take the term "hammer." What is a hammer? According to the Oxford

2. Davidson, *Inquiries*, 247.
3. Ibid.

English Dictionary it is "an instrument having a hard solid head, usually of metal, set transversely to the handle, used for beating, breaking, driving nails, etc." But of course a moment's reflection shows that such a definition has a limited usefulness. If I am looking for a hammer in my tool shed with someone who did not know what a "hammer" is, could he use such a definition to assist me in finding a hammer? Suppose he asks me, "what are you looking for?" and I say "a hammer." "What is that," he replies, and I say, "An instrument having a hard solid head, usually of metal, set transversely to the handle, used for beating, breaking, driving nails, etc." This definition does help us some. It helps us recognize that a hammer is not a basketball. The information has some usefulness; it narrows down which objects in my tool shed fit the category and can even help us start our quest for the hammer in a general direction, but it would not help him determine what we are looking for. A number of objects might fit this definition—a hoe, hatchet, pickaxe, etc. I can always further clarify the definition until he realizes which object fits it, but even in this case, the definition has a limited usefulness. It only helps us find an object when someone had no idea what it was. This seldom occurs and is a strange way to think about how we normally learn and use language.

We seldom learn language by matching definitions with objects in the world. For the most part, we already "know our way around" in a language long before we learn, or construct, definitions of terms. We learn language through participating in everyday activities that require an understanding of the terms in order for us to know "how to go on." These are acquired habits and skills about which we can become self-reflexive, but we do not have to be so in order to have them. Think how odd it would be if you were roofing with someone and you call out to her, "give me a hammer," only to get the response, "what exactly do you mean by 'hammer'? Do you mean an instrument having a hard solid head, usually of metal, set transversely to the handle, used for beating, breaking, driving nails, etc.?" How could you make sense of such a strange question in the midst of an activity like roofing? You would think she is crazy, pulling your leg, or showing off her knowledge of dictionary definitions. But you would not assume she is engaging well in the activity of roofing. Her question shows that she does not understand "how to go on" when a roofer calls out to his partner, "give me a hammer."

Language makes sense only within the context of everyday activities that we do not so much invent as inherit. I doubt that many people learned the term "hammer" because someone gave them a definition of it, and yet we know how to use it in a number of diverse contexts even when the term has different meanings. One such meaning is the example just cited above where someone is engaged in an activity and asks for a hammer. But if we are at a football game and watch someone get hit and say "he got hammered," we recognize that the term "hammer" is used similarly, yet with significant differences to how we used it while roofing. When I ask my brother to "give me a hammer" on a roof I am not inviting him to do to me what happened to this player in a football game. Because I know he is able to use language in this flexible manner I can fearlessly cry out to him "give me a hammer." The meaning of the term is defined by its use, and knowing the appropriate uses is as important as knowing what the words themselves mean. If this is true of an ordinary term like "hammer," how much more is it true of a metaphor like culture.

Many discussions of theology and culture begin with a definition of culture. H. Richard Niebuhr did this in his well known book, *Christ and Culture*, which is one of the most important works on our topic. He stated, Culture is "that total process of human activity and that total result of such activity to which now the name culture, now the name civilization, is applied in common speech. . . It comprises language, habits, ideas, beliefs, customs, social organizations, inherited artifacts, technical process and values."[4] This definition is helpful. Culture is a "human activity." It is similar to the term "civilization." It relates to "language." But how much work does this definition actually do? It does have its uses. It distinguishes culture as a human activity from forms of activity that are other than human. It assumes a clear distinction between nature and culture as well as between human and divine activity. It points us in a general direction. Yet opposing culture to nature still requires more analysis for the term nature is as complex as the term culture. Nature can mean:

1. the essence of a thing which makes it what it is, as in "the nature" of humanity or "the nature" of song;

2. the human participation in God's eternal laws, which was known as the "natural" law and was available to all without the divine law given by the church;

3. the result of God's act of creation;

4. the state of being without grace;

---

4. Niebuhr, *Christ and Culture*, 32.

5. an uncultivated state, whether in politics or in bio-
    logical growth as in the expression "a state of nature,"
    or a "natural state"; or

6. fixed laws found in science.

Understanding culture in opposition to nature makes our
task more difficult because of these diverse understandings
of what we mean by "nature." The line between nature and
culture is not easy to draw, which does not mean it cannot be
drawn at all. Because the laws of physics or logic are natural
and not human developments, they could be exempted from
Niebuhr's definition of culture. Likewise theology based on
divine activity rather than human activity could be other than
culture. In fact, Niebuhr has to distinguish "culture" from
"Christ" in order to compare and contrast them. Christ represents something other than culture; he is eternal and exempt
from human making. This is what allows him to be related
to "culture," which represents temporal, human activities. We
will return to a discussion of Niebuhr's *Christ and Culture*
below. For now, the key point is that while a definition of
the term "culture" is certainly helpful, like a definition of the
word "hammer," it only points us in a direction. To understand best what we mean by culture we will need to examine
how the term gets used.

Questions for Reflection

1. What is culture?
2. How would you explain "metaphor"? Give some examples of everyday metaphors.
3. What is nature?
4. How might culture and nature relate?

Confusing Nature and Culture

Do Niebuhr's distinctions between natural and human, and between human and divine activities help us understand the relationship between theology and culture? For better or worse, what may have appeared as clear boundaries to Niebuhr in the 1950s are no longer so clear. Films like *Artificial Intelligence: AI* and *The Matrix* blur the boundaries at the level of "popular culture." Movements such as post-human evolution consciously merge human nature and cultural technological products. What appears natural is now nothing but an artificial intelligence, a cultural product. Correlative to this "boundary confusion" at the level of popular culture are the confusions noted by contemporary philosophers and theologians. For instance, the philosopher Slavoj Žižek takes something as natural as defecation and its disposal in everyday life and shows that even though everybody does it, everybody does not do it in some common, universal way. The cultural and ideological differences found among "German reflective thoroughness, French revolutionary hastiness" and "English moderate utilitarian pragmatism" can be found in how each constructs lavatories.[1] German, French, and English lavatories represent these cultural differences. If something this "natural" contains cultural significance how clear is any distinction between nature and culture?

Science, sex, reproduction, and religion are all now viewed by many as inextricably defined by culture. As the theologian John Milbank puts it, "our perceptions of nature and culture seem to be merging." We humans no longer think of ourselves as bound by "natural law." Where people once studied so-called "laws of nature" to know how to act politically and morally, we no longer think such laws are just there waiting to be discovered. Many, if not most, philosophers now think of these laws as "projection by humans upon nature in general."[2] We give nature its order. As one of the greatest philosophers of the Enlightenment, Immanuel Kant (1724–1804) suggested, the advance of science works on the premise less that our mind conforms to nature and more that nature conforms to our mind. Modern life increasingly views "nature" as a cultural projection. We can make and remake nature into what we think it should be. This is true of biology, reproduction, and nearly everything we once understood as "nature." Through the dominance of technology, nature and culture merge. I discovered this when I remarked to someone how thankful I am that the city of Chicago, where I live, "preserved" a natural forest right through its middle so that we bicyclists can enjoy riding through the woods. But then I discovered that our "Forest Preserve" is not that. No forest was ever preserved; it was fabricated through reclaiming land and replanting trees at a date long after indus-

1. Žižek, *The Plague of Fantasies*, 4–5.
2. Milbank, *Being Reconciled*, 188–89.

trialization had cleared all the forests in the Chicago area. Is it natural or cultural?

While our times are characterized by recognizing "nature" as a "cultural" process, at the same time they also paradoxically view "culture" as an increasingly "natural" process. Our "aberrant" behavior is viewed as a medical condition remedied through medication. Some in the post-human evolution movement even find our thoughts to parallel those of the binary logic of computers so that it may be possible to download them into a supercomputer and give us a virtual eternity. We live in strange times where culture becomes nature; nature becomes culture. Everything is a sign, but we have little to no control over the signs' effects in our lives. In such a world how can we distinguish nature from culture?

Just as the nature/culture distinction seems to come undone, so does the human/divine one as well. This has negative and positive consequences. In much of modern thought "God" is nothing but a projection of the collective human will. Theology is anthropology, which suggests that when we speak about God we are unwittingly doing nothing more than speaking about human being. Some of the most important "fathers" of the modern era, Ludwig Feuerbach (1804–1872), Karl Marx (1818–1883), Friedrich Nietzsche (1844–1900), and Sigmund Freud (1856–1939) basically saw our use of the term "God" as a cultural achievement and/or product that says more about us than it says about God. It names our own powers from which we are alienated, or it names powers we wished we had, but do not. If this is true, if theology is anthropology, then it would make it difficult to do theology at all. Yet there is a positive understanding of this as well; one that fits quite well with the Christian story of the incarnation where God assumes human nature. As the Catholic theologian Karl Rahner stated, theology is anthropology when anthropology is understood as Christology. Since Mary's *fiat*, the boundary between human and divine activity has been blurred.

Mary's *fiat* is the Latin word for her response to the angel Gabriel when he announced "you will conceive in your womb and bear a son, and you shall call his name Jesus." Mary responded, "let it be to me according to your word." This response begins in Latin with *fiat*—"let it be." It is the "cultural" condition for the possibility of the incarnation. Without Mary's *fiat*, without her language of consent, the incarnation does not take place. In other words, human cooperation makes God present in the world. This is witnessed to in the odd Christian doctrine of the *theotokos*, which literally translated means "God bearer." Mary births God.

Of course, this has to be rightly understood. It too is a metaphor and could easily lead to the wrong assumption that humans have a titanic power to make gods present at their command—something like the old sitcom *I Dream of Jeannie*, where Larry Hagmann rubbed a bottle and out popped Barbara Eden to fulfill his wishes. The doctrine of *theotokos* is not that kind of paganism. The church's confession says that Jesus as truly God and truly human was "born of Mary the Virgin, who is God-bearer [*theotokos*] in respect of his human-ness." This confession is, like all Christian doctrine, a cultural artifact that helps us speak well about a mystery. Does the ability to speak in this way blur the distinction between "human" and "divine" activity? Does it make it impossible to distinguish human culture from divinity? Not really, for the church also confesses that in Jesus, God is God and humanity is humanity without division, separation, confusion, or transmutation of the two natures. What does this mean? It means that in Jesus God remains God and humanity remains humanity, but they act as one because they are now found in one person. Jesus is not two persons—one human and one divine—he is one person who is perfectly two natures—divinity and humanity.

The church's confession, as well as postmodern developments that blur nature and culture, human and divine activity, for better or worse, should caution us against any fixed definition of culture that sets it against nature or pits human against divine activity. What then does this tell us about culture? The meaning of culture is not found in a precise definition, but in the various uses for the term.

The ability to understand how language functions in given contexts is a function of what we mean by the metaphor "culture." But this is complicated because what is true of the term "hammer" is also true of the term "culture." It should not be treated as if it is a secure, definitive something that gives us the condition for the possibility of knowing other things, but not itself. In other words, "culture" is not a distinct foundation upon which other things like "language, habits, ideas, beliefs, customs, social organizations, inherited artifacts, technical process and value" build. Unfortunately, given the popularity of the term "culture" today, it often functions like this kind of foundational condition for the knowledge of other things such that once someone appeals to "culture" they have not opened up the possibility of conversation but foreclosed it. Culture functions like a secure foundation that somehow gives meaning to other things—even God. The argument "that is my culture" or "that is their culture" supposedly renders actions intelligible. But that would be a strange use of the term "culture," much like saying that an "instrument having a hard solid head, usually of metal, set transversely to the handle, used for beating, breaking, driving nails" is the foundation for understanding the activity of "hammering." "Culture" does not explain anything; at its best it should invite us into a conversation about how and why we engage in the activities we do. When "culture" forecloses that argument rather than opening it up, it no longer functions as a metaphor. Instead it is being used as nothing but a blunt instrument.

Questions for Reflection

1. Do you find nature and culture merging in our post-modern times? Do you see this as promising, perilous or both?

2. Can we still distinguish nature and culture? What is a natural activity free from culture? What is a cultural activity distinct from nature?

3. How do we distinguish human and divine activities?

4. How do human and divine activities become one in the Christian tradition?

4

Language

The above discussion gives some hint to the complexity involved in using the term culture. Given this complexity why should we try to relate theology and culture at all? As we already noted, we have no choice. Once God calls Abraham and Sarah to be God's people, once God tells Moses to speak to Pharaoh, once Mary says yes to the angel's pronouncement, once God becomes incarnate, etc., theology is cultural. Most theologians have always known this and it is why they have traditionally been so attuned to the importance and complexity of our use of language. H. Richard Niebuhr understood this when he defined culture as comprised of language. But this emphasis on culture and its relationship to language was intensified once an important event took place in philosophy known as the "linguistic turn." To understand why contemporary theologians are so preoccupied with questions of culture also requires some discussion of this important event.

Culture matters because our knowledge is inseparable from our language, and our language constitutes, in part, what we mean by the metaphor culture. Without the philosophical turn toward the significance of language, we modern theologians would not be preoccupied with culture. To understand why we have become so preoccupied with it, we must explain what has become known as "the linguistic turn." If there had been no "linguistic turn" in philosophy, we theologians would most likely not be as interested in the question of the relationship between theology and culture as as we have been since the second half of the twentieth century.

What is the "linguistic turn"? It is the assumption that intractable questions in metaphysics and theology, questions such as:

- Is there a God?
- Are we free or determined in our actions by natural forces?
- What is true, good and/or beautiful?
- What does it mean "to be"?
- Is there a distinction between the world as it is and the world as my mind represents it?

cannot be solved without an examination of the language used to describe them. For thousands of years philosophers tried to give answers to these questions, but were unable to offer satisfying answers that resolved them in most peoples' minds. The "linguistic turn" was an effort to look less at the "things in the world" or the "concepts in our minds" in order to seek answers to these questions, and instead to examine the language we use in speaking about such things. Many thinkers who made the linguistic turn thought it dissolved the questions metaphysics raised, or reduced them to manageable themes that language could address.

Although the movement known as the "lingustic turn" began long before that term was specifically used to describe it, the term itself was first used by Gustav Bergmann in his book, *Logic and Reality* in1964. He stated, "Much of the paradox, absurdity and opacity of prelinguistic philosophy stems from failure to distinguish between speaking and speaking about speaking. Such failure or confusion is harder to avoid than one may think. The [linguistic] method is the safest way of avoiding it."[1] In other words the intractable problems of philosophy can be remedied not by trying to figure out the relationship between "concepts or universals" and the "things" intended by these words, but by tending to the words themselves, by speaking about speaking. For the "linguistic turn" philosophical and theological problems can be better understood—if not resolved—if we think of them not so much as metaphysical problems that seek to discover some kind of entity, but as problems of language; for no matter what we say about the "somethings" these problems raise—it can and will only be said in language. So the way forward in making sense of these intractable problems is to be attentive to language and how it is used. What will this accomplish? Although we cannot agree about what, or if, God, being, freedom, nature, truth, goodness, beauty are, we may explicitly or implicitly agree on the language we use to speak about these matters.

The claims made by philosophers who find a complete break between philosophy before and after the "linguistic turn" are overdrawn. Attention to language can be readily found among philosophers and theologians prior to the linguistic turn even though they did not think attention to

1. See Rorty, *The Linguistic Turn*, 8–9.

language alone could resolve metaphysical disputes. Given the track record of philosophy after the linguistic turn, we should not be romantic about its ability to solve these issues either.[2]

Of course, nearly every philosopher has recognized, to some degree, the importance of language. Take Aristotle's definition of truth: "To say of what is that it is not, or of what is not that it is, is false, to say of what is that it is, or of what is not that it is not, is true." This basic definition of truth brings together language and "what is" and correlates them. The true is what corresponds to the things language tries to signify. This is often called a "realist" or "correspondence" theory of truth. But what Aristotle meant by this definition is not easily determined. Did he mean truth is primarily a matter of rightly labeling things in the world, as if the work of truth were to go about putting "sticky notes" on things, matching "what is" with "what we say about it"? If that were the case then truth would be nothing more than getting the right term for the right thing. As long as I call the "coffee cup" before me "coffee cup" and not "bicycle" then I recognize the truth of the matter. But is this an adequate account of truth and language and was Aristotle so silly as to suggest such a thing? Of course it is very useful for me to know that my coffee cup is not my bicycle, especially when I want to drink coffee or ride my bike, but such a simplistic account of truth does not help us explain well how we use the term. When my wife says, "that is a beautiful sunset," and I respond "that is so true," I do not mean by true something as mundane as the fact that her words matched the thing.

2. See my *Speaking of God* for a more extensive critique and discussion of the linguistic turn(s).

I don't think that Aristotle or most realist and correspondence accounts of the truth are as simple minded as the above description of them suggests. They assume much more than the "sticky note" approach to language and things. But this is often the way they are characterized, both by their supporters and their detractors. Yet an effort to seek to discover truth by simply relating the right proposition to the thing to which it refers did characterize some of modern philosophy and theology. This effort did not require the significance of culture in order to understand anything. It assumed we could build a universal, neutral, and objective way of signifying things so that everyone would have an equal access to what is irrespective of their culture or language. "Culture" (and language) emerged as an important element in our thinking when Johann Georg Hamann called this (supposed) universal and objective way of knowing into question. Hamann (1730–1788) is part of a tradition in Germany—along with Johann Gottfried Herder (1774–1803) and Wilhelm von Humboldt (1767–1835) —that also underwent a "linguistic turn." Hamann thought the German Enlightenment wrongly separated sensibility and reason. It tried to answer questions by having us bracket out our sensibilities, passions, culture, language, etc., abstract from them, and remain neutral and objective. To understand anything well we had to distance ourselves from a passionate attachment to it and approach it as neutral observers. Hamann thought this was not only vain, but false because of the importance of language. He wrote, "Not only does the entire capacity to think rest on language, but language is also in the middle of the misunderstandings of reason with itself."[3]

3. Quoted in Edwards, *Encyclopedia of Philosophy*, 4:407.

Language always already projects itself in every situation, allowing us to understand anything. This is both the possibility for understanding and misunderstanding.

Hamann opposed Immanuel Kant's efforts to establish science on grounds of "pure reason." He did not think reason could be "pure" because of its association with language. Kant thought reason could be pure of tradition and belief, everyday experience and language.[4] Hamann disagreed. But if reason was not pure, if it was inextricably connected to these three, then it could not escape "culture." As Cristina Lafont puts it, "once we accept the symbolically mediated character of our relationship with the world, we cannot avoid the problems posed by the contingent and determinative character of the world view transmitted in and by language."[5]

Johann Gottfried Herder drew on Hamann's work and broadened our understanding of how "culture" worked. For some philosophers, language and culture could mediate reason, but they did so through a progressive realization where what was true emerged in what was called "civilization." Such people were willing to acknowledge that our reason was mediated through language, but they assumed Western European civilization was the apex of that progressive realization. Herder objected to this and stated:

> Men of all the quarters of the globe, who have
> perished over the ages, you have not lived solely to
> manure the earth with your ashes so that at the end
> of time your posterity should be made happy by
> European culture. The very thought of a superior

4. Lafont, *Linguistic Turn*, 7.
5. Ibid., 37.

European culture is a blatant insult to the majesty
of Nature.[6]

After Herder we no longer speak of "civilization" or "culture," but "cultures." Yet this does raise certain problems, even if they may finally be pseudo-problems. The problems it raises are these:

1. If our understanding is mediated through language and culture, and cultures and languages differ, do the world's cultures and language groups share different understandings of the world?

2. If we share different understandings of the world, are they so different that we could not even understand one another? (This is the problem of incommensurability discussed below.)

3. How can we adjudicate among these different, and possibly incommensurable, understandings if any attempt to adjudicate among them will itself be one more understanding mediated by language and culture?

4. Can we speak intelligibly of anything outside our culture and language?

5. This raises the significant problem of the question of the relationship between theology and culture. If God can only be spoken about in terms of the different languages and cultures of the world, then is God anything other than a product of our culture and language?

6. Williams, *Keywords*, 87.

What are we to make of the linguistic turn? Can we make it and still do theology? Does it dissolve theology like it supposedly dissolved the philosophy known as metaphysics? Does it make us relativists such that to make the linguistic turn is to forego any sense of theological unity when speaking about God? Can we still be theologians after the linguistic turn? Can we still speak of God? Before we tackle these questions, it might help to see how the discipline that studies "culture" most directly, the discipline of sociology, addresses some of these difficult questions.

Questions for Reflection

1. How does language relate to culture?

2. If our understanding is mediated through language and culture, and cultures and languages differ, do the world's cultures share different understandings of the world?

3. If we share different understandings of the world, are they so different that we could not even understand one another?

4. How can we adjudicate among these different, and possibly incommensurable, understandings if any attempt to adjudicate among them will itself be one more understanding mediated by language and culture?

5. Can we speak intelligibly of anything outside our culture and language?

6. This raises the significant problem of the question of the relationship between theology and culture—is God anything other than a product of our culture and language?

Diverse Uses of "Culture"

Raymond Williams was largely responsible for the development of a discipline known as "the sociology of culture." It is now a flourishing discipline taught in the academy and used by corporations, churches, the government and the military. Of course they do not all use its findings the same way. Take for example the church. Some people use the findings in the sociology of culture to market religion to various identified "cultures" like baby boomers, generation xers, the millennium generation, etc. Here sociology of culture develops broad, generic categories as to how entire generations supposedly think and act. Others use the same findings to decry such usages. This helps illustrate another key point Williams made. He not only argued that the term "culture" is problematic because of its transition from a "noun of process" to a "metaphor," but also because as a metaphor it functions differently among and within disciplines. In other words, the term "culture" does not function in the same way in biology, philosophy, sociology, anthropology, or theology, even though it is used in all those disciplines. What a sociologist like Max Weber meant by "culture" is radically distinct, and perhaps even incompatible with what someone like Raymond Williams meant by it. The term "culture" gets used in diverse ways even within the discipline of sociology.

One of the important questions in analyzing any use of the term "culture" is to ask whether it is best understood through "thin" or "thick" descriptions. A thin description seeks to discover the bare minimum that needs to be said in order to understand "culture." Its purpose is to make a culture intelligible based on universal laws that anyone could understand. It wants to maximize understanding among as many diverse people as possible through succinct, simple, and potentially universal statements. A thick description assumes no such universal laws are possible. Instead, a culture is best understood by standing within it and explaining its richness through something like a narrative that invites others into the culture. If "culture" is presented in terms of universal laws the term is being used markedly different than when it is presented in terms of narratives. The social sciences employ two different interpretive frameworks in order to present these "thin" or "thick" descriptions. The first is called "nomothetic" and the second "idiographic."

The term "nomothetic" comes from two Greek terms: *nomos*, which means law, and *thesis*, which means position. A nomothetic interpretation of culture seeks to discover the laws from the perspective of a universal position which would allow anyone to understand the metaphor of culture. In other words, it assumes someone could stand in a netural space and observe how cultures function without becoming a participant in that culture itself. A nomothetic interpretation seeks to understand culture in terms of objective, universal laws that anyone could understand. It reads the "culture" by standing "external" to it. Idiographic also come from two Greek words: *idios*, which means peculiar to one's self or private, and *graphē*, which means a mark. In opposition to a nomothetic interpretation of social reality, an idiographic one looks for the peculiar marks within a culture in order to understand it.

A nomothetic reading of culture works much like a scientist who tries to build the proper instrument for observing some object. The observation requires the discovery of universal laws. For instance, in my college biology class we spent a great deal of time observing whether certain flies had red dots under their wings. We counted the wings with dots and those without, tabulated the findings and correlated them, and then tried to develop laws which would help us make sense why it was that some flies had the red dot and others did not. (Of course, in our case we already knew the answer and hoped our observations would fit what we already knew.) Is the metaphor of culture to be rightly understood through a similar means? Should we stand outside a culture like a scientist, collecting data, making neutral observations, and not allowing our prejudices to obscure the findings? A famous example of this would be James Frazer's *The Golden Bough* where he tried to understand a "primitive" culture's use of magic from a "rational" and "universal" perspective. The result was that he could only see the use of magic as an earlier (inaccurate) version of modern science. Magic was understood as a form of pseudo-science such that when social communities understood how science worked, they would abandon the earlier culture, which depended on magic. A "magical" culture was interpreted in terms of a "scientific" culture where the latter was thought to possess the kind of universal, neutral rationality that could function as an objective instrument that would make sense of a more "primitive" culture based on magic. This leads to what are known as "thin" descriptions of social reality.

An "idiographic" understanding of social science, however, assumes that one has to stand within a culture to understand it. To use another metaphor, to understand why the fly really has the red dot under its wing, I would have to be more than an observer, I would have to get inside the fly's "culture" and participate in it. Where the "nomothetic" seeks to avoid prejudices and thus offers the bare minimum in terms of how to understand social reality, the "idiographic" must give rich, detailed historical narratives in order to make sense of it.[1] It requires "thick" descriptions. Of course, both approaches have promises and limitations. Take the example of an effort to understand a snake-handling church.

What would it take for me to understand what is going on in a church where one of its essential practices is snake-handling? Can I stand back and simply observe, take notes, and seek to offer an adequate explanation for what is going on in terms of observable, neutral universal laws? Should I be committed to a position of neutrality, refusing to be taken in by the trance like state snake-handling preachers can produce in their followers? Or is such a position of neutrality possible? Will whatever language I use to explain why some people handle snakes in church always come already with some kind of evaluative connotation? Take for instance the expression

1. I am indebted to Charles Taylor for much of my understanding of how the social sciences work. See especially Taylor, *Philosophy and the Human Sciences*.

I just used—"Trance-like state." Is that a neutral description or an evaluation? It is not how these persons would describe themselves. They would understand their actions as gifts made possible by the Holy Spirit who protects them as Scripture states when Jesus says, "these signs will accompany those who believe: . . . they will pick up snakes in their hands, and if they drink any deadly thing, it will not hurt them" (Mark 16: 17–18 NRSV). Should we observe the culture of a snake-handling church by ridding ourselves of all prejudices in an effort to present their own description of what they do? Should we observe snake handling churches with an open mind, or should we observe them by bringing with us some prejudices? And if so, which ones? Should we assume certain common, universal psychological laws as to what it means to be a healthy person, which normally excludes handling snakes or drinking poison? Or should we adopt a fundamentalist reading of Scripture that would be open to the possibility that snake-handling is a valid sign of belief in order to understand this odd practice?

Perhaps I need to enter into the culture of snake-handling myself in order to understand it. But once I have entered into this kind of reality, will I lose any ability to stand outside the culture and explain it to others? Will I lose any external reference point? Answers to these questions will depend on what purpose our explanations and/or descriptions of a culture serve. If we approach "culture" as a social scientist who seeks to understand why people handle snakes and drink poison on their own terms, our answers will go in the direction of presenting the culture in their own words. If we approach it as a psychologist who wants to understand certain pathologies, our answers will go in a different direction. And if we approach it as theologians, pastors, or religious people who seek to understand who God is and how we relate to God, answers will go in yet another direction. In each of these cases "culture" will be used differently. The very disciplines we use to approach and understand culture will bring with them a set of questions and assumptions that are inescapable. No approach to "culture" can avoid this, even though the "nomothetic" seeks to minimize the questions and assumptions as much as possible. This is why the linguistic turn and culture are so important. They show us that we are always making some kinds of judgments when we observe phenomena.

The nomothetic approach to understanding social reality has the advantage of offering universal explanations that anyone could understand whether or not they ever handled snakes. But it has the disadvantage of always keeping our understanding of any social reality at a distance, as if we were looking at life through the safety of a Plexiglas window. This raises the question whether such an objective stance is truly objective, or whether it sneaks in somebody's interpretive lens, somebody's culture. The idiographic approach tries to "get inside" a culture in order to understand it. But it can assume that cultures are incommensurable, which is to say that the boundaries around a culture are like impermeable membranes which one cannot break through unless one becomes a cultural insider. The nomothetic approach "stands outside" a culture in order to understand it. But the distance it posits could prevent it from understanding the culture, assuming that observation rather than participation gives persons access to all that attends the metaphor of "culture." So whereas the nomothetic assumes that cultures are too transparent, too readily observable to an outsider, the idiographic assumes they are too opaque and only accessible to the insider. Both views have limitations. The nomothetic approach leads observers to fail to see how they import their own cultural assumptions into their observations. They mistake their own position as universal and fail to see it as one more particular culture. The idiographic approach, however, can emphasize participation to such an extent that it ends in solipsism where each culture is viewed as walled off from others, unable to communicate outside its own cultural framework. Taken to an extreme, the nomothetic assumes a complete translatability among different cultures whereas the idiographic assumes a complete incommensurability, which means that nothing in one culture can function as a criterion or measure for something in another culture. Here translatability is impossible.

Both solipsism with its incommensurability, and universalism with its complete translatability, are impossible positions to sustain. One need not worry about them because no one can actually adhere to either one of them except in terms of a theory that does not actually do any work in the real world. Too much misunderstanding occurs among and within cultures for anyone to assume they have mastered the universal rationality by which they always work, or for anyone to even assume there is such a universal rationality just waiting to be discovered. Likewise too much everyday basic communication and exchange occur among and within cultures for anyone to seriously sustain the charge that they are completely incommensurable. To begin any analysis of the metaphor of culture by assuming they are either completely translatable or incommensurable is to begin at the wrong place. Questions about how to understand culture should not begin with either assumption, but with conversations with other cultures recognizing that no understanding can take place if we are not all standing somewhere. To posit a "neutral" space outside "culture" where any culture can be objectivity delineated is difficult, if not impossible to maintain for that supposed position will only have access to "culture" through language, customs, beliefs, practices, etc. Cultures can certainly engage with one another, but they do so only because all the participants are standing in some culture.

Let me offer an example. Some years ago my wife and I were missionaries in Honduras where I was a local Methodist preacher and she ran a medical clinic among a people called the Guarifuna. We lived in an area with a high infant mortality rate. One of the reasons for it (at least from the perspective of a scientific culture) was dehydration that occurred among infants because they became ill when they drank formula mixed with water from a contaminated supply. (The fact that babies were fed infant formula rather than breast milk, and that my wife and I were missionaries in this place, already reveals that Guarifuna culture was not something closed off from anything external to it.) However, when the babies would become dehydrated the Guarifuna women referred to it as "mole drop." Their explanation was that the babies' brain had slipped and to save the baby they had to get the brain back into position. To do so they would make a paste and apply it to the top of their head or sometimes hold the baby upside down. My wife would regularly teach in the clinic that this was a mistaken remedy. What the babies needed, she argued, was rehydration. But this did not make sense to many of the Guarifuna people and we were unable to get them to come to the clinic when the baby had "mole drop" because they did not find the language of "dehydration" compelling in explaining what had occurred. Was there something in the Guarifuna culture associated with mole drop we did not understand? Was "mole drop" the same thing as "dehydration"? Did we have incommensurable languages and cultures that prevented communication?

When I was in graduate school at Duke University I use to tell this story to discuss the practical effects of claims by some theologians and philosophers that the reality of every culture was constituted by the language available to it. We were quite taken by the importance of language and culture for how one could understand any reality and the example of "mole drop" seemed to show its significance. In one sense, calling this reality "mole drop" or calling it "dehydration" had real, concrete, practical significance. "Mole drop" had one remedy; "dehydration" had another. We all understood certain terms—brain, slip, thirst, hydration, etc. But how they were related differed. The way the language was put together produced different realities, different human activities. But how different? The remedies for mole drop did not work; babies died. Rehydration worked; babies lived. I remember becoming disillusioned with the strong, incommensurable thesis some of my fellow students advocated when it seemed to ignore this reality. They suggested that the use of "mole drop" by Guarifuna culture had its own reality that no one could understand without adopting that culture and language to such an extent that one had to be convinced that the remedies for mole drop were preferable, or at least as reasonable, to those of rehydration. In other words, the truth of the reality of "mole drop" is so relative to the Guarifuna culture that unless one truly came to embody the "mole drop" language, one would not understand how these remedies actually did work. One day a fellow student pressed me with the question, "But did not the remedies for mole drop work within the Guarifuna culture? Was it not a form of unwarranted coercion to try to convert the Guarifuna from the language of 'mole drop' to that of 'dehydration'?" At that point, I became disillusioned with any strong thesis for incommensurability; it denied the significance of everyday life.

Does this mean that we can define "mole drop" in terms of "dehydration" without remainder? This assumption of a completely translatable culture from one to another is also unwarranted. Tradition, practice, social conventions were all associated with the diagnosis and remedies surrounding "mole drop." To adopt another language completely would be to lose those practices, including the role of women healers within the Guarifuna culture. To "convert" persons from the language of "mole drop" to "dehydration" required understanding how and why the term "mole drop" functioned as well as a compelling account of why the term "dehydration" could do all "mole drop" did and more. This was possible precisely because cultures are not incommensurable. It was necessary because cultures are not transparent and completely translatable. For the same reason it was difficult and could never be decisively accomplished. It required openness to the other culture at the same time that one tried to make sense of it in terms of one's own culture and understand one's own in terms of the other.

Neither the assumption of incommensurability nor that of a complete translatability helps us understand well how culture functions in everyday life.

Questions for Reflection

1. Does the distinction between nomothetic and idiographic accounts of culture help us understand its diverse uses?

2. How is it possible to understand another culture?

3. When do we assume cultures are easily translatable into each other?

4. When do we assume cultures are incommensurable?

5. How might you respond to the "mole drop" example?

6. Several years ago, while working in Appalachia, someone with whom I was working stated that he went to a holiness church and hoped one day to become sufficiently holy that he could handle snakes without getting hurt. How would you respond to such a statement? Should you leave your prejudices behind when seeking to understand this person's "spirituality"?

6

Culture and God

Applying the metaphor of culture to human beings and our
social relationships is exceedingly complex. How much more
complex matters become when we apply it not only to human
beings, but also to our relationship to God. Yet the pervasive-
ness of the term "culture" in contemporary theology could
cause us to overlook this complexity and think someone has
done something significant simply because he or she invoked
the term "culture." Everyone seems to think they know what
they mean when they say "culture," and thus it is readily invoked in all kinds of theological discussions. But what does it
mean? Can the metaphor be clarified? Or will the very clarifi-
cation ruin the metaphor? What is the process of cultivation
when applied not to soil but to people in their encounters
with God?

The interactions between Guarifuna culture and my
own western, scientific culture were similar to the interactions
that occur everyday in my work as a theologian. Theology is
a science of human action that seeks to understand who God
is and how God relates to us and to creation. However relating this human activity, which is theology, to God is much

more difficult than relating Guarifuna and Western culture; for God is not an object in the world to which we can refer. Yet if we cannot refer to God, if we cannot intend to speak about God, where "intend" has the meaning of tending toward something, then how is it possible to do theology at all?

Theology is always done in and through language and that makes it specific to a culture. Think for a moment about these various terms:

> God, Gott, Deus, Dieu, Allah, Yahweh, Goddess
>
> Father, Son, and Holy Spirit; Creator, Redeemer, and Sustainer
>
> *Theos*, Dios, Dio

Each of them intends to present in language an "object" for theology. Do they all "refer" to the same thing? Since none of these terms refers to a "thing" that is an object in the world that can be pointed to and followed by exclamations that designate it such as "there it is," "here it is," "this is it," etc., how could we possibly answer the question if they all "refer" to the same "thing"? To what then do they refer?

Most of us who believe in God do not think these terms refer only to the concrete, material token (i.e., the mere letters G-o-d inscribed or uttered somewhere). What we mean by "God" is not the letters g and o and d spoken, written, carved, or otherwise marked. Speaking, writing, carving, marking those letters somewhere is a cultural phenomenon of our own making. But when we engage in such a cultural activity we assume that it contains something more as well; that it intends a reference beyond the mere speaking, writing, carving, or marking of those three letters. Nor do we assume that these terms refer to some virtual reality like the term "unicorn" does. I think I understand what is meant by "unicorn," the object to which it refers has a kind of existence separate from the mere collection of letters u-n-i-c-o-r-n so that I can teach my children how to recognize "unicorn" from "donkey," even though I know it has no actual existence. I cannot take my daughter to ride on the unicorn at the local petting zoo. U-n-i-c-o-r-n, as an assemblage of letters, functions similar to s-a-n-t-a-c-l-a-u-s-e. Both refer to something other than their tokens, even if that reference has no actual existence. This differs from the assemblage of marks 'vm-a;sdlv'ktb;luvfi', which I produced by typing randomly on my keyboard. It refers to nothing but a mere collection of random marks on a page. It has no reference beyond itself.

When theologians use terms such as God, Gott, Deus, Dieu, Allah, Yahweh, Goddess, Father, Son and Holy Spirit, Theos, and Dios, we recognize that we are engaged in a cultural activity, but we usually do not use these terms as simply an assemblage of marks that refers to nothing but itself. We intend to express something beyond the tokens themselves. Nor do we mean a collection of marks that point to some virtual reality like "unicorn" or "santa clause." Of course, the term "God" can be used in these ways. Think of Nietzsche's claim "God is dead and we have killed him." How is "God" being used here? Did Nietzsche actually think God was once a living entity but now that living entity no longer exists? Of course not. Claims like Nietzsche's can only use the term "God" as a human projection of a virtual reality that we use for our own sake. For Nietzsche, theology is anthropology (and not Christology.) The death of God implies that we no longer need to project this token—G-o-d—onto any reality in order to make sense of our own lives. We can live just as well without G-o-d as we did with G-o-d. Some theologians (they are usually referred to as atheologians) do use the terms with only these linguistic references, but that is not the way most of us use the term. We would never confuse the bare collection of letters G-o-d with what those letters signify. As Thomas Aquinas, an important thirteenth-century theologian put it, how we signify (the use of a language in history in a given cultural context) can never be identified with what we signify—the reality we call "God." (The first he called the modus significandi or the "mode of signifying"; the second the res significata or the "signified thing.") Nevertheless how we signify intends or reaches toward "something" actually signified. Does this then mean I can use any language whatsoever to refer to God?

This is something of a controversial question among contemporary theologians. I certainly cannot use just any term and expect people to understand me, for instance, I cannot call God "tuna," "Bod," or "The Entity Formally Known As." If I am leading worship and say "the tuna be with you" or "the One who cannot be named be with you" people in the congregation would not know how to respond. But how constrained are we in speaking of God? The terms God, Gott, Deus, Dieu, Dio, and Dios may be replaceable, but can they be replaced with Father, Son, and Holy Spirit? Can they be replaced with Mother, Child, and Spirit? With Allah? or Yahweh? How would I know that what we are talking about (res significata) remains the same when I change how I speak about it (modus significandi), which inevitably occurs?

Simply because I recognize a distinction between the "mode of signifying" and "the signified thing" does not mean that I am at liberty to use any language I want. The example above shows that language depends in part on its use in a community. "The Lord be with you. . . and also with you" helps Christians name the specific God whose name we invoke before we pray. But is this purely arbitrary? If I garnered sufficient agreement could I replace the term "Lord" with some other? How can we humans speak of God, if we can at all? This question is the question of theology and culture; for every answer to the question of theology—the question "can we speak of God?"—has also become, for us modern and post-modern people, a question about culture. Why has it become a question of culture? Language itself is now understood primarily as a cultural activity. After the philosophical and cultural assumptions of "the linguistic turn" how we speak is a question of this metaphor of "culture." Theology is always, at least in part, a question of how we use language. Theology and culture have become inextricably linked.

Rather than answering precisely how we can speak of God given the central role culture plays in theology, I will now examine how different theologians and different schools of theology use "culture" to speak of God or to limit others' claims about how they can speak about God. This may be all I am finally capable of doing, not because I don't think we can speak about God. We do that all the time through worship, prayer, preaching, teaching, and writing, and we do it without finding it to be problematic. The fact that we are not able to give a precise explanation how we do it does not change at all the fact that we do it. Nevertheless, by showing how other theologians use the term "culture" in doing theology, we might gain some clarity in how this is done, even if we will never achieve precision. I finally think precision is impossible and unwarranted because our speaking about God functions "analogically" or in terms of "family resemblances" where we find ourselves saying "it is something like this." I think this is warranted by the incarnation itself where God is found in human form as One Person with both human and divine natures without mixing or separating humanity and divinity. I am convinced that our question—how do we relate theology and culture?—is ultimately one of our answers to Jesus' question to his disciples and to us, "who do you say that I am?" In other words, the answer to this question will depend on who we think Jesus is. If we do not find him to be One Person who is both divinity and humanity, then we will not need to see the close relationship between God and culture as human making. This would be the heresy known as Nestorianism where Jesus is both divine and human but he is not sufficiently One Person. Likewise, if we do not maintain the distinction between divinity and humanity we will absorb God into human making without remainder. This too would be heretical. Interestingly, the best answer to the question of the relationship between theology and culture is to be found in an orthodox Christology.

Questions for Reflection

1. To whom (or what) do we refer when we use the term "God"?

2. Where are those places in the church's life where we use this term without finding it in the least bit problematic?

3. Under what conditions do we find reference to "God" to be a problem?

4. How might you respond to those persons who think that our use of the term "God" is nothing but a projection of our own wishes and desires on an empty space?

5. How does the orthodox understanding of Jesus as One Person who is both humanity and divinity, and yet divinity and humanity remain distinct, help us think through the questions of the relationship between theology and culture?

7

Theologians and Culture I:
The Work of Ernst Troeltsch

When theologians such as Paul Tillich, H. Richard Niebuhr, George Lindbeck, James McClendon, Katherine Tanner, Sara Coakley, or John Milbank (all of whom we will discuss below) use the term "culture" they not only give it a different significance than the sociologists and philosophers, they also differ among themselves in their use of the term within the discipline of theology. For instance, Tillich and Niebuhr see culture as a source separate from theology to which theology must be correlated. This requires a "correlational" theology where both culture and theology engage each other as different kinds of entities. Lindbeck, however, sees culture as a term internal to theology. He could not "compare" theology to culture because this would be akin to comparing triangles and a three-sided planar figure whose angles always add up to 180 degrees. Both these schools of theology make the metaphor "culture" central to their understanding of theology, but differ greatly in what that means.

Whenever we theologians discuss the relationship between theology and culture, we tend to fall into some well-worn patterns. This is inevitable; we are always dependent upon the work that was done before us and a great deal of work on this question was done in the twentieth century. That work often used the terms "culture" or "civilization" (the metaphors are similar) as juxtaposed to terms such as "theology," "faith," or "church." It begins by asking the question: "What is the relationship between Christ and culture?" Or it asks another version of this question: "What is the relationship between the church and the world?" One of the first theologians to ask and address these questions was Ernst Troeltsch. He published an important two-volume work in 1911 titled *The Social Teaching of the Christian Churches*. Anyone who seeks to understand well how theology and culture have been related in the twentieth century should begin by reading through this important work.

Troeltsch drew on the work of the social scientist Max Weber, especially how he related ethics and politics. Weber stated that all ethical action was guided by either an "ethics of ultimate ends" or an "ethic of responsibility," but only an ethics of responsibility was "political." This is because an ethics of ultimate ends refuses to calculate the consequences of one's actions. This kind of ethics is found in Jesus' teaching on The Sermon on the Mount. In contrast to it, an ethics of responsibility does estimate "foreseeable consequences." It recognizes that an "absolute" ethic can never be faithfully lived out in history if someone or some group seeks to make a contribution to politics. Weber stated unequivocally, "The decisive means for politics is violence." If someone lived by an ethics of ultimate ends like Jesus' teaching in the Sermon on the Mount, then he or she would be required to renounce violence. In renouncing violence one would also be renouncing politics.[1]

Troeltsch developed something similar to Weber's ethics of responsibility and ethics of ultimate ends in his claim as to how the church relates to culture. Troeltsch did not find the "original idea" of Christianity to be particularly social, political, or cultural. It was, as he put it, "purely religious." For that reason Christianity was asocial and apolitical. Because it was asocial and apolitical Christianity could not survive in human history without help; a purely religious idea required some social embodiment for its own continuation—it needs "culture." This meant that Christianity required a relationship to central social institutions that were the "main formative powers of civilization," which for Troeltsch were the state and society. By society he meant economic relations not regulated by the state. Therefore, Troeltsch used the term "civilization" within the context of a question, "How can the Church harmonize with these main forces in such a way that together they will form a unity of civilization?"[2] The Gospel as a religious idea required expression through these other "main" forces that produced social movements, particularly the state and society. If the church was to be social, it could only be so through its connection with these two social institutions. This established the dominant use of the term "culture" and its relationship to theology within the twentieth century. The question of "theology and culture" is now used to ask how the church can cooperate with state and society to serve some

---

1. Weber, "Politics as a Vocation," 119–21.
2. Troeltsch, *The Social Teaching of the Christian Churches,* 1:32.

greater end than all three possess alone—that greater end is called "civilization" or "culture."

Troeltsch developed three typical answers to the question how theology and culture related: sect, church, or mysticism. The *sect* type seeks to preserve the theological integrity of the religious idea by rejecting and standing against the formative social institutions of the state and society. It preserves the original purely religious idea, but it does so through social and political irrelevance. However, the preservation of a purely religious idea is impossible; it cannot survive without some connection to the main formative social institutions of civil society and the nation state; it must inevitably bow to them for its own survival. Troeltsch thought churches like the Anabaptists embodied the sect-type approach. The *church* type adopts the form of those formative social institutions and mimics their structures, but in so doing it loses the religious idea. The Roman Catholic Church, especially in the Middle Ages, represented for Troeltsch the church-type. It took on the trappings of the Roman Empire; the emperor became the pope; the Roman Pantheon became St. Peter's Basilica. The result was a social and historical institution that could preserve its own culture, but at the expense of the theological integrity of the religious idea.

The third type—the *mystic* type—was for Troeltsch the clear preference, and the one that he thought would be the legacy of the Protestant Reformation as it mixed with modern culture. Troeltsch defined mysticism as "the insistence upon a direct inward and present religious experience."[3] It reacts against "objective" institutional forms of Christianity medi-

3. Ibid., 2:730.

ated through institutions, tradition, dogma, ritual, etc. in favor of an immediate experience of the divine. But like the sect type, the mystic type cannot sustain itself without some institutional structure such as the church type. Although it is closest to the purely religious original idea of Christianity in its valuation of the individual, it needs the church type for its own continuation.

These three types can be categorized as follows:

Theology's Social Context	Church Type	Sect Type	Mystic Type
How is the Church formed?	Objectively through the sacraments	Subjectively through voluntary commitment	Inwardly through personal experience
What is the Church's identity?	It is an institution endowed with grace and salvation as the result of Christ's work, which it now has authority to dispense. Thus it practices infant baptism.	It is a voluntary society only for true believers who have made a commitment to the gathered community based on 'the new birth'. Thus it practices believer's baptism.	The true church is a "mystical fellowship" that cannot be defined by any formal worship or doctrine. It is only defined by a "purely personal and inward experience." Baptism is relatively unimportant.
How is Christ mediated to the world?	Through the Church and the sacraments	Through the gathering of the voluntary community	Through an "inward spiritual principle"

| What is the Church's relationship to culture? | The Church has an obligation to take *responsibility* for the larger culture. It does this by availing itself of all the political, social and cultural means that it can. For this reason, warfare is permissible. | The sect *withdraws* from the larger culture. For the sake of the purity of the Gospel, it refuses to dirty its hands in social, cultural and political matters. It refuses to participate in warfare. | The mystic type neither takes direct responsibility for, nor withdraws from, the larger culture, but it cultivates the inward life producing a "factor in the universal movement of religious consciousness in general." |

This grid reflects Troeltsch's use of the term "culture" as it applies to theology. It is not an uncontested appropriation of that term, which we will note below. I present it not because I think it is persuasive in its answer to the question, "What has theology to do with culture?" but because it has been so influential in framing other answers to the question.

Troletsch concluded his two-volume work with a section called "Christianity and the Modern Social Problem." This is a return to the question that began his work, "How can the Church harmonize with these main forces [state and society] in such a way that together they will form a unity of civilization?" He left us with an either-or, for he suggested that only "two great main types of social philosophy attained comprehensive historical significance and influence." That is to say, only two answers to the question as to how the church relates to culture have endured. The first is "Medieval Catholicism." The second is "Ascetic Protestantism," which encompasses both the sect and mystic-type. The former bases relationships on "personal relations of authority and reverence" while the latter bases them on "the responsibility of the individual and the duty of love."[4] Troeltsch thought both these "powerful types have now spent their force." Neither one will work in the new context of the modern age with its culture so vastly different from Medieval or Reformation culture. A new type must emerge, and Troeltsch does not detail what that new type will be. He only tells us that something new is necessary to address the never before seen rise of "modern" culture, although he does imply it will look something like the mystic type.

The cultural type of Christianity that will address this new modern social problem had not yet been thought when Troeltsch wrote his 1911 work, but he did imagine that this new type will emerge from the pieces of failed Christian social teachings found in the remnants of both Medieval and Reformation culture. It will seek to establish its "ideal," but like those earlier forms it too will fail; for, Troeltsch concludes, no such ideal can ever be actualized "within the sphere of our earthly struggle and conflict."[5] In other words, the answer to the question how theology relates to culture never ends. Theology always tries to give an answer and to actualize its answer in an ideal situation, but the messy temporal realities of everyday life always prevent its actualization. Each answer fails, only to give rise to new answers, which will themselves inevitably fail as well. This is Troeltsch's legacy and I will call it the legacy of the "liberal Protestant" tradition. We shall see

4. Ibid., 2:1011.
5. Ibid., 2:1013.

the influence of this legacy in two other of the most important theologians who correlated theology and culture: H. Richard Niebuhr and Paul Tillich.

Questions for Reflection

1. Troeltsch found in the Gospels a "purely religious idea" that was not in itself social or political. To what extent do you find this persuasive?

2. Do Troeltsch's three types—church, sect, mystic—seem plausible? Do they help illumine the Roman Catholic or Anabaptist churches as you have experienced them? What might be the limitations on this typology? How might you find it persuasive?

3. Why did Troeltsch think we can never finally answer the question as to the relationship between theology and culture?

4. Should the church contribute to something called "culture" by joining forces with civil society or the nation state? In what ways might this be possible? In what ways impossible?

8

Theologians and Culture II:
H. Richard Niebuhr's Typology

Troeltsch's work set the stage for nearly every consideration of the relationship between theology and culture that followed. His legacy includes a twofold concern that preoccupies much of modern theology: 1) what is the relationship between Christ and culture broadly considered; and 2) what is the relationship between Christ and the specifics of modern culture.

Troeltsch's legacy can be found in two important theologians who addressed how we relate theology and culture broadly conceived: H. Richard Niebuhr and Paul Tillich. We will look at Niebuhr in this chapter and Tillich in the next. These theologians sought to address the question of culture broadly considered; that is to say, they did not address more specific questions like how we relate theology to "local cultures" of North American—"baby boomers," "Gen-Xers," or "the millienium generation"—or how we do theology in the era of Starbucks coffee (and the myriad of other kinds of modern cultural moments to which theology and church life now seek to correlate themselves). It might be, however, that those more specific correlations of theology to culture, which preoccupy so many church leaders, are species of the generic question of theology and culture that Niebuhr and Tillich so powerfully addressed. In other words, if we had not first become preoccupied with the question how theology and culture relate, we would not be so focused on the more specific question of "local" cultures. We might not be so preoccupied with finding sociological generalizations of large swathes of people and movements and then attempting to make theology relevant to them. It is a peculiar feature of our modern culture that we are so driven to find characterizations of it and then claim we must be relevant to those characterizations. This may be indebted to H. Richard Niebuhr's and Paul Tillich's emphases on "culture" as one of the correlates theology must address if it is to speak to modern people.

Two of the most important theological uses of culture are found in important works by H. Richard Niebuhr and Paul Tillich. Niebuhr published his well known-book *Christ and Culture* in 1951, and Tillich published his *Theology of Culture* in 1959. To say that Niebuhr and Tillich influenced nearly every theologian who correlates theology and culture would only be a slight exaggeration. The importance of their work cannot be underestimated. However, they both depended upon the earlier work accomplished by Ernst Troeltsch and Max Weber. Without Troeltsch and Weber, Niebuhr and Tillich's theology of culture could not have been produced.

H. Richard Niebuhr provided one of the most important and long-lasting answers to the question how theology and culture relate to each other by expanding on Troeltsch's typology. He was deeply influenced by Troeltsch, who was the subject for his doctoral dissertation. He took Troeltsch's three basic types and expanded them to five. They are:

1. Christ against Culture
2. Christ of Culture
3. Christ and Culture in Paradox
4. Christ above Culture
5. Christ the Transformer of Culture

These five types are Niebuhr's description of how theologians address what he calls the "enduring problem," which is how Christ and culture, or Christ and civilization should relate to each other. The problem is this: Christ represents the mediation between the eternal, which is outside of time, and the historical, which is in time. Culture and civilization represent historical, and therefore finite, limited achievements. Bringing them together can lead to an unstable blend of the eternal and historical. The temptation is either to collapse the eternal into the historical or collapse the historical into the eternal. The first temptation makes Christ merely a representative of culture. The second destroys culture by either setting Christ against it or preserving him from it. He is preserved from it when he is placed in a paradox with it or set above it. We avoid these temptations only when the eternal constantly transforms the historical without either collapsing one into the other or keeping them from each other.

Niebuhr explained these five types, offered examples of key religious persons who loosely fit within each of them, and then offered criticisms of four of the five types. He did not offer any substantive criticism of the middle type, "Christ the transformer of culture." The following table shows his analyses:

Type	Examples: people	Examples: churches	Key Features	Problem
Christ against Culture	Tertullian, Tolstoy	Mennonites or Anabaptists	Christ is set against culture. The Christian rejects any loyalty to culture in favor of Christ's sole authority over the Christian.	This position is honorable but impossible. Loyalty to Christ cannot be had without the mediation of culture
Christ and Culture in Paradox	Luther, Kierkegaard	Lutherans	Christ is set over and against culture, but not as a rejection of culture. The two live together in a paradox. They cannot be harmonized.	This position embodies a cultural conservatism that changes religious institutions without changing cultural ones.
Christ the transformer of Culture	Calvin, Edwards	Reformed, Presbyterians, Baptists, Methodists	Christians seek to transform the culture.	No problems are associated with this position.
Christ above Culture	Thomas Aquinas, Pope Leo XIII	Roman Catholics, Anglicans	Christ, represented by the category "supernature," is set above the category "culture," which is represented by the term "nature."	This position refuses to face up to the "radical evil" that is always present in culture.

Christ of Culture	Gnostics, Abelard, Kantians like Ritschl and Schleiermacher	Modern Protestants	Christ and culture are not set in opposition. They exist in a harmony.	This position fails either to be loyal to Christ or to meet the demads of culture.

The usefulness of Niebuhr's types have been questioned by many persons who represent church traditions other than the Reformed theological tradition established by John Calvin, which Niebuhr found to be the most preferable of the five types and called "Christ transforming culture." Mennonite Christians do not take kindly to being called apolitical and sectarian these days. Some of them have lived between enemy camps in difficult places like Palestine, Latin America, and Iraq. They ask why they are thought to "withdraw" from culture simply because they refuse to take up arms. They have taught us to question whether both Troeltsch and Niebuhr's typology works only when we begin with Weber's claim that politics is violence.

Likewise many Roman Catholics find the interpretation of their tradition as defined by a rigid distinction between nature and supernature to be a distortion. This interpretation suggests that "grace" is something simply added onto nature without actually being integrated with it. Much of Catholic theology before and after the important Second Vatican Council (1962–1965) worked diligently to reject this caricature of the Catholic tradition. During this time many Catholic theologians rejected an earlier doctrine of "pure nature," which assumed that the human being could exist without grace in a state of pure nature. They suggested all human nature was only possible when it received something that was more than human nature itself. Niebuhr interpreted Catholic theology in terms of this pure nature and rightly criticized them for it. He did this before the Second Vatican Council changed things. Yet Niebuhr's own definition of culture never escaped the old doctrine of "pure nature" for he defined "culture" as a thoroughly human making. If "culture" is nothing but a human activity, then it is already understood as distinct from grace, from God's transcendence, or from what came to be known as "supernature." In other words, "culture" is not a gift to be received from God outside of immanent human activity; it is only what we human creatures do. Then Christ, like grace or supernature, will have to be added on to an otherwise completely human activity called "culture." This notion of "grace" can only function as "extrinsic" to nature, never fully integrated with it. Twentieth century Catholic theologians such as Henri de Lubac and Hans Urs von Balthasar challenged this very interpretation of Catholic theology, which drew on the thirteenth century theologian Thomas Aquinas for support.

De Lubac and von Balthasar's adversaries called their theology a "new theology" (it usually goes by the French term "nouvelle théologie"). This was a term of derision intended to castigate their theology as being "new" or "modern." Because theology helps us understand an ancient revelation, to call what theologians do as "new" or "modern" is usually an indictment against them. The "nouvelle théologie" took the name, but rejected its meaning. They understood that theology can never simply be "new" or "modern" because it is always based on a revelation that occurred at a particular time in the past and is mediated through history. To make it modern or "new" in a profound sense would require an act of forgetting, forgetting the witness of all the previous Christians who assist us in faith. Far from accepting that they were offering a "new theology," or thinking this was a virtue, they understood their work as a return to the earlier sources of Christian theology. But they reread those sources without thinking that they had to do so in terms of the Scholastic Roman Catholic theology of the sixteenth to eighteenth centuries, which was preoccupied with countering the Protestants. In particular, they reread the theology of Thomas Aquinas and offered a different interpretation than the Scholastic interpretation one finds in Niebuhr's *Christ and Culture*. In fact, their reformulation integrates theology and culture more closely than even Niebuhr's efforts to do so through his "Christ transforming culture." Their efforts led to some of the key revisions that took place in the Roman Catholic Church during its Second Vatican Council.

The Second Vatican Council was called by Pope John XXIII and closed by Pope Paul VI. In one sense, it was an effort to "update" the Roman Catholic Church to modern culture. The term used for this was *aggiornamento*, a Latin term that means "to bring forward." It can also be loosely translated as "accommodation." The Protestant theologian Karl Barth was an observer at Vatican II, and he asked the Catholics an important question based on their use of the term *aggiornamento*. He asked, "What does *aggiornamento* mean? Accommodation to what?"[1] The basic answer to his question was "to modern culture." This was important because Roman Catholic theology had rejected much of modern culture as incompatible with the Christian faith. However, at Vatican

1. Rowland, *Culture and the Thomist Tradition*, 19.

II, official Catholic teaching began to speak of a "right to culture." This led to changes such as the development of national councils of bishops; these did not exist prior to Vatican II. They were an effort to help the church respond to the local cultural context within which it found itself. They also did away with the use of the Latin language in worship in order to use the vernacular language of each culture. Where once all Catholics heard the worship in a common language (even if they could not understand it), now they hear it based upon the language of their ethnic or national culture. Although many of these reforms began as an effort to overcome a sharp distinction between theology and culture, or grace and nature, in Catholicism, they have now become controversial in some quarters. Some Catholic theologians seek to take the reforms further and emphasize the local cultural context more and more. Others think that the consequence of these reforms has been the loss of a distinctly Catholic culture and its dissolution into ethnic and national cultures which is more characteristic of Protestant than Catholic Christianity. Some argue for an "autonomy of culture"; others argue that this idea has become a repetition of the very doctrine of pure nature that defined scholastic theology and that Vatican II sought to remedy. One cannot understand the political and cultural significance of the Catholic Church today without recognizing the importance of these debates about how the church should think of theology and culture. Niebuhr's typology does not always help us recognize the complexity of this important debate within Catholicism.

Besides the limitations posed in the descriptions of the various positions that come from the Anabaptist churches like the Mennonites and the Roman Catholic tradition, Niebuhr's types only work if we accept two important theological themes: that Christianity is primarily about a "permanent revolution," and that Christianity presumes a "radical monotheism."

Niebuhr sets up the problem of Christ and culture as a variation on the problem of how to relate the eternal and the temporal. As a theologian working in the Reformed tradition he seeks to preserve God's sovereignty and transcendence from any reduction to immanent human powers. Niebuhr takes this so far that he argues Christianity entails a "radical monotheism" where nothing finite and historical can finally represent the eternal. God is radically transcendent; God stands against all representations of God in space and time. This honors the first three commandments, as we noted in the beginning of this guide. Niebuhr makes no graven images of God. But Niebuhr takes this so far that he even states Christians must never confuse the Lordship of God with the Lordship of Christ. This is what he means by "radical monotheism." For Niebuhr, the significance of Jesus is that he points away from himself to God. Because of this radical monotheism, the Reformed Christianity Niebuhr represents requires a "permanent revolution." (This is similar to Paul Tillich's "protestant principle, which we will discuss below.) Christ as the eternal mediates culture through historical, temporal manifestations. But every historical and temporal manifestation of the eternal Christ, including that of Jesus of Nazareth, is inadequate precisely because it is historical and temporal. This leads to the need for a permanent revolution where we never accept any temporal presentation of the eternal Christ, but must permanently transform them in terms of whatever culture we find ourselves. As we shall see, this fits well with modern culture and that moment known as the "end of modernity."

Culture functions here as the temporal, historical mediation of the eternal Christ that can never be adequate to what it mediates. But this could be a misleading use of the term culture that overlooks some of the important theological claims in the Christian tradition whereby even the truth of theology is a human making, as we mentioned with the doctrine of the incarnation, Mary's role as *theotokos*, the preaching of the Word, the sacraments, and the church's conciliar deliberations that produced our orthodox doctrines of who Jesus is. In other words, these "cultural" makings, which are also gifts received from God, make God present in the world. Moreover as the Mennonite theologian John Howard Yoder recognized, Niebuhr first creates a "monolithic" definition for culture and then rigorously relates theologians such as Tertullian, Schleiermacher, Aquinas, Luther, and Calvin to that monolithic definition. Whether or not his definition functions to illumine well these various theologians is not a question he raises because he makes his definition of culture the standard to which theology must be measured. Can culture be used as an external standard of measurement for theology? This use of culture is quite similar to that of another influential mid-twentieth century theologian, Paul Tillich.

Questions for Reflection

1. How helpful is Niebuhr's typology?

2. Does Niebuhr's typology help us understand what we mean when we use the terms "Christ," "Church," and "Culture"?

3. Should theology seek to be new and relevant?

4. How is Mary's giving birth to Christ a "culture"?

5. Is preaching and/or the celebration of the Lord's Supper a "culture"?

6. Should theology correlate itself to "culture"?

9

Theologians and Culture III:
Paul Tillich's Protestant Principle

Paul Tillich, more so than any other twentieth century theologian, used the relationship between theology and culture as the means by which to update theology for modern times. Tillich argued that theology works by correlating itelf to culture. Culture poses questions that it cannot answer itself; theology provides answers, but each of those answers is given in a cultural form, which then raises further questions. Theology's answers seek to relate culture to God, or the "ultimate concern." But every time it does this it does so through means that are less than ultimate by the very nature of their finite, historical forms. These means can only offer a penultimate concern. Tillich explained this as follows, "Religion as ultimate concern is the meaning-giving substance of culture and culture is the totality of forms in which the basic concern of religion expresses itself. Every religious act . . . is culturally formed."[1] Theology provides answers to the questions culture poses, but every answer it provides will inevitably be an expression of a culture in a particular time and place.

1. Tillich, *Theology of Culture*, 42.

Therefore theology's answers to a culture's questions become themselves cultural artifacts that raise new questions which theology must answer anew. This process goes on indefinitely such that no answer can ever be sufficient. Everything must always be subject to critique, revision and new presentations, which themselves will then be subject to critique, revision and new presentations, which themselves will then be subject to critique, revision, and new presentations.

Tillich called this "the Protestant principle." He offered different definitions for it, but its basic meaning can be found in his statement, "one can only speak of the ultimate in a language which at the same time denies the possibility of speaking about it."[2] Tillich's claim is similar to that which we discussed above in Thomas Aquinas; there is always a difference between the way we speak about God (*modus significandi*) and that about which we speak—God (*res significata*). The former will be a cultural "artifact" or a human making found in time and space and thus inevitably cultural. But there is also an essential difference between Tillich and Aquinas. For Tillich the distinction between how we speak of God and what we speak about "denies the possibility" of speaking about God. Every utterance about God fails, and we know this before we even begin to speak. For Aquinas, this distinction does not insure than we cannot speak about God for he is less certain than Tillich as to what our language can and cannot accomplish. We can still speak about God; language does not fail in the same way that it does for Tillich.

Tillich's work has the distinct advantage of highlighting the importance of cultural context for theology. Both his and

2. Tillich, *The Dynamics of Faith*, 60.

Niebuhr's claim that theology cannot but be cultural should be noncontroversial. Who could deny this? All theology depends on a cultural context. In fact, many theologies that we now call "contextual" assume Tillich's basic theological framework. They seek to show how theology will be a function of context. Take for example James Cone's work emphasizing the cultural context of African-Americans in the United States for theology.[3] By showing us how the church contributed to and was silent before the normativity of Black suffering, Cone shows the relevance of cultural context both for "white" and "black" Christianity. His early work draws heavily on Tillich's theology of culture for its inspiration. Other contextual theologies have done the same for women, Latino/as, and other marginalized and dispossessed groups. Tillich's theology is not the sole cause for these theologies, but it is no surprise that many of the early pioneers in these contextual theologies drew on his work with its emphasis on cultural context. They could have drawn on a number of theologians in the tradition. Most reasonable theologians have always recognized they face an arduous task in using the limits of language to express what is without limits, the Living God. We moderns did not discover this, but we have tended to turn it into a limit that not even God can transgress, and this does make some claims about cultural context lodged in modern times difficult to sustain. They suggest an unsupportable cultural relativism, which is often called fideism.

In one sense, the claim that theology is always dependent on its cultural context is unquestionably true. We know

---

3. See Cone, *A Black Theology of Liberation*; Cone, *The Spirtuals and the Blues*; Cone, *Black Theology and Black Power*.

this from the "linguistic turn." Whatever language we use to speak about God comes from a particular, cultural context. Even the English I use in this book differs radically from the English used by Julian of Norwich in her theology. If I used her old English it would be difficult for you to understand what I write. I would not know how to do that; nor would I be tempted to do so. Who would be tempted to use Julian's Old English to write theology for today? It would be too much work. This raises the question once again, do we have any choice but to write theology in our given cultural context? If not, why is this set forth as a revolutionary claim in so much of modern theology? When theologians emphasize the cultural context of all theological works, whom do they oppose? Are there theologians out there who intentionally are writing in alien cultural contexts?

Theology cannot be the simple repetition of specific ancient linguistic forms even within the same language because it differs over time and space. Yet the claim that theology is "dependent" on its cultural context can become problematic when it sets forth a relativism that suggests cultural contexts are incommensurable across time and space. This kind of cultural relativism comes in two forms. First, it suggests that one *historical* context is so radically different from another that the claims made by an earlier time cannot be measured in our time. We supposedly have to be relevant to our time at the expense of earlier times because we have no access to things people of an earlier generation thought or said because we use a different language to express it. Second, it suggests that two simultaneous *cultural* contexts are so radically distinct that no communication can occur between them. Whenever these kinds of unwarranted claims are put forward, readers should not be unduly troubled. Most philosophers and theologians think such claims are unreasonable; they are difficult if not impossible to sustain.

Sara Coakley is one such theologian. She offers us some useful diagnostic questions to determine what kind of relativism is implied by our insistence that theology depends on cultural contexts. She suggests that we examine such claims in terms of five variables, and argues that an analysis of those variables will show that some of the claims for cultural relativism are "dead ducks," which is to say that when such claims are made they don't have life; they don't get up and walk anywhere. The five variables are:

1. "the status of any given relativism," which should cause us to ask, what kind of relativism is being advocated?

2. the "sphere or realm of discussion," within which "the relativism is deemed to apply." This causes us to ask, is the claim to relativism about our knowledge (truth), our morality (good), or aesthetics (beauty)?

3. "further distinctions" in the category of knowledge when someone makes claims that our knowledge (truth) is relative. This causes us to ask, to what extent is someone claiming our knowledge is dependent upon its cultural context?

4. the "notion of truth" present in a relativistic knowledge claim. It leads to the diagnostic question, what kind of truth claim is made by someone advocating relativism?

5.   the notion of a "cultural or historical framework." If we claim that the truth of our knowledge is dependent upon a cultural or historical framework, then what do we mean by the term "framework"?[4]

These five variables with their diagnostic questions are immensely helpful in clarifying claims about the relationship between theology and culture. Let us examine them more fully.

Coakley's first variable concerns "the status of any given relativism." When confronted with a claim for relativism one should ask what is the status of the claim? Many claims for "relativism" are really something less sinister; they are claims about "relationism." Relationism suggests that our location in space and time bears on our truth claims. This is unquestionably true. For instance, I write the sentence, "I am at my computer working." This is true when I write it, but most likely it will not be true when you read it (especially if you read it past 9:00 p.m. [CST] when I am normally asleep). Coakley calls this the "truism of context." No one should deny this kind of contextual relativism. If all that is meant is this kind of relationism, it causes no concern—of course our historical and cultural context bears on our truth claims. However, she suggests that there is a stronger claim for "contextual relativism" that is problematic.

Drawing on the work of the social scientist Peter Winch, who first advocated this kind of cultural relativism in his 1958 work, *The Idea of a Social Science*, she defines the problematic relativism as "relativism proper" or "epistemological relativism." The word "epistemological" refers to how it is that we

4. Coakley, "Theology and Cultural Relativism," 225.

know what we know. Epistemological relativism suggests that *the truth* of what we know is relative to some cultural framework. This is a stronger claim than simply suggesting that what we know relates to a cultural framework or that our historical and cultural framework will bear on our claims for truth; it suggests something more—the *truth* of a claim *depends* on that framework and there is no way to adjudicate its truth outside of that framework. What does this mean? Recall the story I told earlier about "mole drop." Strong epistemological relativism would suggest that "mole drop" will be true in terms of the framework of Guarifuna culture and if one is not inside that culture one cannot recognize its truth. Is such a claim supportable?

This kind of strong epistemological relativism leads Coakley to discuss two other variables which should function as diagnostic questions when we think someone is making an argument for cultural relativism. Her second variable considers "in what sphere or realm of discussion, the relativism is deemed to apply."[5] If it is an epistemological claim about what constitutes truth, then it is hard to sustain. But even here we must consider a third variable and examine "further distinctions" with respect to "epistemological relativism." There is a weak version which states that "what is true is true in virtue of a framework." And there is a stronger version that Coakely calls "criterial epistemological relativism." It argues that the *criteria* for a truth claim depends on a framework. No reference outside of a framework exists where such internal criteria could be examined. The truth of "mole drop" and "dehydration" depend upon the different cultural frameworks within

5. Ibid., 230.

which those expressions make sense and we have no criteria to adjudicate between them.

This leads to communication-ending claims such as "it may be dehydration to you, but it is mole drop to me; how dare you impose your culture on me." Of course, that sentence can make sense in terms of relationism, which might open up rather than close down conversation, but it more likely functions as "criterial epistemological relativism," which does not intend any further conversation at all.

Do cultural frameworks entail incommensurable criteria for truth claims? This leads to Coakley's fourth variable, which concerns the "notion of truth" operative in the claim "truth is relative to a framework."[6] Can we know with such certainty that no "external reference" exists outside "cultural frameworks"? The very notion of a "cultural framework" leads to her final variable—another "dead duck." What do we mean by a "cultural framework?" Are they distinct spaces like automobiles with tinted windows traveling on the highway where no one can peer into another's autonomous space without first getting into that space? But surely if cultures were like this, communication would not only be difficult, but impossible. Such strong claims for a cultural framework are difficult, and I think impossible, to sustain. This is not to deny the importance of the relationship between theology and culture. It is to place it in proper perspective, to make claims that do not deny what occurs in everyday life. People communicate even when philosophers and theologians cannot account for how it takes place, or when they try to make problematic what is not a problem.

6. Ibid., 233.

Neither Troeltsch nor Niebuhr's types assume a problematic cultural relativism. If they are used to support it, they are being poorly used. Nevertheless, Troeltsch's three and Niebuhr's five types are often presented as neutral sociological types, which is problematic. Many theologians recognize that they are not neutral; they sneak in a specific theological position often called "liberal Protestantism." One should not be confused by this name; it does not mean "Protestants" who are liberals. Instead, it means Protestants who think that the church's task is first and foremost to influence the policies of the *modern* nation-state and civil society by correlating the faith to them. In other words, the tradition of liberal Protestantism assumes that Christianity and modern culture are compatible, or can be made compatible by updating Christianity. It is preoccupied with modernity, which is defined by an insistence on "liberation" or "liberalism." It seeks to bring Christianity and this liberalism together even though there may be some tensions between them. As a tradition, "liberal" Protestantism argues that the church must be free from the past, free from any ancient commitments to ritual, tradition, dogma, or a unifying institutional authority in order always to be flexible in adjusting to new cultural developments. I could call this tradition "free" Protestantism, but that might imply I meant a tradition of a non-established church (i.e., a church that is not supported and sanctioned by the state, a practice that is called "establishment"). The tradition of liberal Protestantism does not preclude establishment, it only precludes seeing the church itself as a society, as a culture that bears a political identity through time.

The identity of the church is largely derivative in liberal Protestantism; it gets its identity by its relationship to civil society and the nation state whatever forms they take. Thus this tradition is preoccupied with those relationships. Here movements on the political right, such as the Moral Majority, and on the left, such as the Rainbow Coalition, even though they have very different policy prescriptions, represent two variations of the tradition of liberal Protestantism. When President Ronald Reagan referred to the United States of America as a "city set on a hill" (he was not the first President to do so), he also stood within this tradition. But for persons who do not find the liberal Protestant tradition persuasive, that reference is deeply problematic. The phrase "city set on a hill" is actually a biblical reference that refers neither to the state nor society but to the church (Matt 5:14). It is a city that bears an identity across time and space, which does not depend on either its opposition to or affirmation of formative cultural societies for its own existence. A theologian or Christian can only find this expression compelling as a reference to the state of society if he or she is already standing firmly in the tradition of liberal Protestantism.

This raises an important consideration in any discussion of theology and culture. Are we discussing theology and culture or are we discussing theology and *modern* culture? I noted above that Troeltsch concluded his discussion of the relationship between theology and culture by claiming we needed a new theology in order to accommodate modern culture. Niebuhr and Tillich both responded to Troeltsch's call by trying to present that new theology. This leads to an interesting irony in contemporary theology now that we may find ourselves in something called "postmodern culture." Niebuhr and Tillich's effort to engage modern culture may have become somewhat "conservative" efforts to preserve it; whereas the "new theology" of de Lubac and von Balthasar, because it never sought to be new, may be the very thing that will help us avoid being captive to a modern culture that has become increasingly problematic. This is why an increasing number of contemporary theologians now look to de Lubac and von Balthasar to help us navigate the "transition" from modern to postmodern culture. To understand this, we will need to examine what we mean by "modern" and "postmodern" culture.

Questions for Reflection

1. Do cultural frameworks entail incommensurable criteria for truth claims?

2. Does Tillich's "Protestant principle" make sense of Protestantism as you understand it?

3. What is cultural relativism?

4. Is the emphasis on "context" in contemporary theology and church life a form of cultural relativism?

5. Is Coakely's critique of cultural relativism persuasive?

6. Why are modern persons so interested in culture?

7. Does theology need to accommodate modern culture?

8. Is it correct to call something like the Moral Majority a form of liberal Protestantism?

10

Theology, Modernity, and Postmodernity

What do people mean when they speak of "modernity?" Let me give an example. I was driving in my minivan with my fifteen-year-old daughter listening to the radio when an advertisement came on for a popular television show. It said, "Don't miss this week's episode; the best episode ever." My daughter naively said, "Dad, didn't they say that last week?" To which I responded, "Yes and they will say it next week and the next week and the week after that. . . ." I then went into a long discourse on what philosophers mean when they speak of the "end of modernity," to which she quickly tuned out once the music returned. What is modernity and why has it come to an end? That example illustrates it well. Modernity is the assumption that everything must be new: each episode, each product, each performance is "new and improved," better than the one before. It is so new and improved that it renders the old obsolete.

The term modernity comes from the Latin word modo, which means "now" or "just now." Modernity is characterized by a perpetual preparation for the now, a perpetual change that must always present itself as new and different, even when it is the same old thing endlessly repeated and simply repackaged with minor changes. But what would it mean to live assuming that we must perpetually change to become something new and different that never quite arrives? Such a perpetual now only masquerades as difference; for, a perpetual now that always almost-appears as new, as change, as difference, is really nothing but sameness under the illusion of difference. Modernity is the repetition of sameness under the illusion of difference. In fact, modernity is a strategy of fear that says everything which has come before has not prepared us for this moment, for this "now," this modo—this "just now"—that has almost arrived. If we are to survive we must discard the past and become relevant to the "now," to this moment. Modernity is thus an exercise in intentional forgetfulness as movies like *The Eternal Sunshine of the Spotless Mind* seek to represent. The "now," the present time, becomes the measure against which all things are assessed. It becomes the answer to the question Karl Barth asked at Vatican II, "accommodation to what?" The answer is "to the present, to the now," which seems to be always the answer in much of modern theology and church life and has been for the past three centuries. "We must be relevant to the now." But this creates serious problems for our culture. As St. Augustine recognized time cannot be measured; it has no extension. If the time of the now is to be the measure which we accommodate, what kind of measure could this possibly be? Take a minute and measure "now." How would you do it? It is a measurement of nothing, it is nihilistic. And thus as a measure it judges nothing except for the one single, dogmatic, and unequivocal judgment—we must be relevant to the new that does not exist.

If this is what characterizes modernity, what is "post-modernity?" Here things become exceedingly difficult. Postmodernity cannot simply be the next cultural stage after the modern, the next "new," because the modern is nothing but the assumption that what is coming is always new and different. So if we define postmodernity as nothing but the next "new and different" we are not postmodern, but merely modern yet again. Many people use "postmodern" simply with this modern cultural sensibility. The postmodern is the next cultural stage to which we must make theology or the church relevant. That is unfortunate for it does not adequately characterize whatever usefulness that problematic term—"postmodern"—actually has. Postmodern culture cannot be the next new and improved version of modern culture; postmodern culture is useful as a term only when it helps us recognize what we mean by "modern" culture. Postmodern culture is not anything but the recognition that we can now see what "modern culture" was and is, and can begin to recognize its limits, even if in so doing we cannot completely transcend those limits. Postmodernity is nothing more than the fact that we recognize the "end of modernity," but this is not an end in the sense that it has come to its completion. Modernity can never end. It is more an "end" in the sense of an ever-increasing, ceaseless repetition that has no purpose other than its own repetition. It is an "end" in the sense that one comes to the end of a record playing on an old phonograph that skips and plays the last note again and again and again. Modernity is a broken record you cannot stop. Postmodernity is the recognition that we, that is those of us formed by modern western culture, are fated to replay modern culture infinitely, more effectively, with an ever intensified rapidity until it kills us with boredom.

For those of us living in the twenty-first century, the question of theology and culture has become inextricably related to "modernity." In fact, we now have a distinct discipline in theology called "modern theology." By this term we do not simply mean "contemporary theology," for every theologian is in his or her day a contemporary theologian. This is inescapable. *Modern* theology means much more than contemporary. It means theology which takes the culture of "modernity" into account. In some sense, every theologian working after modernity has to do this. As the Catholic theologian Tracy Rowland puts it, at the end of the twentieth century, the key issue in theology is "not so much whether one is a self-described Protestant or Catholic, but that of where one stands in relation to the *cultural formation* described as 'modernity.'"[1] David Ford and Rachel Muers have collected the various theological responses to modernity in their work *The Modern Theologians*. Ford offers an important introduction to this collection that begins with two presuppositions: 1) Christianity must have "some continuity with its past"; we cannot be Christian if we become so modern that we altogether forget or jettison the past; and 2) we cannot deny that those of us who live after modernity live in a changed context, a context defined by "modernity" that represents "novelty and disruption."[2] Ford characterizes five types of theology based on

1. Rowland, *Culture and the Thomist Tradition*, 12.
2. Ford and Muers, *The Modern Theologians*, 2.

these two presuppositions. The first type would seek a *simple repetition* of the tradition as if modernity never disrupted it. The second type would argue for a *complete capitulation* to the modern spirit without any concern for traditional continuity. These two types look quite similar to Troetlsch's Church/sect and Niebuhr's Christ-against-culture/Christ-of-culture types. However, Ford notes that neither of these two positions refers to arguments any theologian actually makes. They are positions people use against others. They are accusations—"You think theology is nothing but the simple repetition of tradition!" or "You sell theology out to modernity evacuating it of the content of the faith!" They are usually mere caricatures of other theologians' positions; for no theologian would be so silly as to do one of these two things intentionally, which is not to say that we might not do one of them unintentionally or that the implications of what we do could lead to one of these options. Dan Brown's *The Da Vinci Code* would certainly be an example of a complete accommodation to modernity, while his caricature of Catholicism in that novel would be an example of simple repetition. But this is a piece of fiction; it is not theology and should not be discussed as such. Novelists are free to do what they want to entertain us. If we theologians present theology as simple repetition of the past or complete accommodation to modernity that evacuates the faith of content, we fail at our task.

Ford's next three types attempt to categorize various theologians based on their responses to modern culture. His third type gives priority to the *self-description* of the Christian community. These theologians tend to recover the theology of the eleventh-century theologian Anselm or the thirteenth-century theologian Aquinas. Some representatives would be Karl Barth, Stanley Hauerwas, and George Lindbeck. The fourth type seeks a *correlation* between theology and modern culture. These theologians tend to adopt a more positive attitude toward the modern era and seek to address its concerns. Theologians in this category are often called "revisionists." Examples would be Paul Tillich, Edward Schillebeeckx, and Hans Küng. The final type uses some modern conceptuality and seeks to *integrate* Christianity with it. Examples here would be Friedrich Schleiermacher, Rudolf Bultmann, Wolfhart Pannenberg, Karl Rahner, and much of what is called contextual theology. If we placed it on a continuum, Ford's typology of theological responses to modernity lines up like this:

1. Theology simply *repeats* past creedal statements.

2. Theology *privileges* the self-description of the Christian Community over modernity.

3. Theology *correlates* modernity to Christian Theology.

4. Theology *integrates* Christian theology into a modern conceptual framework.

5. Theology *accommodates* Christian theology without remainder to a modern conceptual framework.

Of course Ford's typology has all the limitations of Troeltsch's and Niebuhr's typologies. Many of the persons listed in these various types will certainly balk at their placement just as Mennonites, Catholics, and at least this Methodist balk at their placement in Niebuhr's typology. Yet what I find helpful in Ford's typology is that *verbs* more so than *nouns* characterize it. Ford shows us that theology is less a proper categorization of positions in terms of some "periodic chart of the theologians," and more an activity people do. How they do that activity after modernity differs. Those differences will have significant theological and political consequences, even if those differences are not necessarily incommensurable. Privileging does not exclude repeating, correlating, integrating or accommodating. Correlating does not exclude repeating, privileging, integrating or accommodating and so on. But this does not mean we can simply include all these activities in a smooth harmonious whole. How we begin and execute the activity called theology matters. If we begin correlating rather than accommodating or privileging then we will get a "cultural" product that looks different just as if we begin baking pie with apples rather than peaches we will get something different, although we will not know that simply looking at it from the outside. One has to taste and see.

Questions for Reflection

1. What is modernity?
2. What is postmodernity?
3. Can you give an example of theology as simple repetition of the past?
4. Can you give an example of theology as selling out to modernity?
5. Do Ford's five verbs help us understand how theology deals with modernity?

11

Contemporary Theology I:
Post-liberal, Analytical,
Post-modern Feminist

Of course, Ford's verbs are not the only five "verbs" that characterize the activity of relating theology to modern culture,
but they are some of the more important. I want to conclude
our work by examining six Protestant and Catholic "schools"
of contemporary theology, each of which relates theology and
culture differently. They all offer us an important way forward through our preoccupation with theology and culture,
although some of those ways are more persuasive than others.
I will characterize them as:

1. Post-liberal Theology
2. Analytical Theology
3. Post-modern Feminism
4. Radical Orthodoxy
5. Communio Catholicism
6. Anabaptist Witness

I chose these six because they offer real insight into the question at hand—how do we and how should we relate theology and culture? However, they are by no means intended to exhaust the plethora of movements within theology that address this question. We will examine the first three in this chapter and the final three in the next.

The 1984 publication of George Lindbeck's *The Nature of Doctrine: Religion and Theology in a Postliberal Age* was something of a revolution in our understanding of the relationship between theology and culture. Where Troeltsch, Niebuhr, and Tillich *correlated* theology and culture as rather distinct things, Lindbeck raised the question whether we would better understand theology if we thought of it in terms of a "cultural-linguistic" activity rather than something that had to be related to such an activity. This *privileged* the church's description of what it does. Theology does not begin with the question how can we speak about God and seek to answer that question through means external to how in fact the church does speak about God. Theology begins by recognizing we do speak about God and then asks what the significance of that speech is. If we assume we have a standard greater than the church's actual speech about God, then that standard will be the judge of our theology. It will be more important than the actual language used to do theology.

Lindbeck set his own cultural-linguistic type of theology against two other forms of theology that related theology to culture, which he called "cognitive-propositionalist" and "experiential-expressivist." The cognitive-propositionalist type engages in the activity of theology by describing objects with matching propositions. For instance, the proposition "God is triune" describes in propositional form a being who is objectively three Persons. Lindbeck does not doubt that God is objectively triune, that this language intends to speak about an "object" outside of language, but he questions whether our use of doctrine is that kind of description and propositional activity. He finds there to be too much distance between the language and the "object" to which the language refers in the cognitive propositional approach. In other words, the language matters too little because all it does is stand in as a "proposition," holding a place for the object, which could be known without the language. Language becomes an instrument we use to describe an object. This would be similar to, in an extreme case, the "sticky note" analogy described above.

The experiential-expressivist type also assumes this kind of distance between language and an object. But whereas the cognitive proposition assumed an instrumental use of language where naming an object is *primarily* getting a right description of the right object, the experiential-expressivist type finds language to be almost infinitely flexible. At its extreme a proponent of this school would say that any language about God would do for they are all basically the same. They do nothing but express an individual's experience of God. In defining the "experiential-expressivist" type Lindbeck states, "it interprets doctrines as noninformative and nondiscursive symbols of inner feelings, attitudes or existential orientations."[1] This definition needs unpacking. By doctrines Lindbeck means official church teachings like "God is Triune" or "Jesus is fully divine and fully human in one Person." By "noninformative" the experiential-expressivist implies that doctrines do not actually

1. Lindbeck, *The Nature of Doctrine*, 16.

add anything to our knowledge of God, because the function of doctrine is to "express" a common core "experience" religious people share in common even if they do not share a common language about how to express it. By "nondiscursive" Lindbeck suggests that the experiential-expressivist does not rely on an "integrated network" of language and culture in order to speak or understand well what is meant by the term "God." The term "discursive" assumes that arguments "run along" our use of language. They move from premises to conclusions which become premises that then lead to other conclusions. For this reason the language used matters. But a "nondiscursive" form of reasoning would not make the language used this important. Instead language is primarily decorative; it is more like the wrapping paper that hides a gift and makes it attractive. But the wrapping paper is not itself the gift. You can change the wrapping paper without changing the gift. For experiential-expressivism, theological language does not produce a reality, it only expresses an inner religious, feeling, attitude or orientation of one's being that is there whether one has a language for it or not.

Lindbeck is often criticized for treating religions as incommensurable cultures with impermeable membranes. This is rather ironic given that his development of the cultural-linguistic approach to religion was intended to help us speak across the boundaries of our different churches and religions. If the cognitive-propositionalist is correct, then differences among churches and religions cannot be remedied unless everyone can agree on the right descriptions and convince each other that by these descriptions they intend the same object, which is not likely to happen. If the experiential-expressivist is correct, then the differences among the churches or religions do not really matter. The experientialist-expressivist always already knows we all worship the same God (or gods?) before we even have a conversation about it. Lindbeck does not think we can move the cultures of the churches and religions forward with either of these options. He is a Lutheran theologian who began his career as an observer at the Roman Catholic Second Vatican Council. He is an "ecumenical" theologian, which means that he very much wants to find a way that the church can come back together into a unity and also have a meaningful conversation with the other religions that does not assume our two impossible positions of solipsism or incommensurability. The purpose of his cultural-linguistic approach to doctrine is to navigate between a cognitive-propositionalist refusal to recognize the legitimacy of other church's teachings—as for example when Protestants reject Catholics because of the teaching of the infallibility of the Pope or when Catholics reject Protestants because of their teaching that "only the Bible" can be the authority of the church—and the experiential-expressivist indifference to doctrine. He thought he could do this by arguing that doctrines function more like cultural languages than propositions in our mind or mere expressions of religious experiences that can be named anyway someone chooses.

In the cultural-linguistic model, the church's teachings are thought to "resemble" languages. It is important to note that Lindbeck does not say the church's teachings *are* languages, he says they "resemble them." What does that mean? *This means that doctrines communicate kind-of-like languages where content and rules of grammar work together to convey meaning.* They function like "idioms for the construing of reality and living of life."[2] Let me give an example. Take the following important statement; read it through quickly and then read it more carefully until it begins to make sense:

> .*content where communicate together—languages of*
> *convey that like doctrines mean rules grammar kind*
> *This and help meaning work to*

No matter how many times, nor how carefully, you read through the sentence above in italics, it will never make sense. Astute readers will recognize that it contains every word in the previous italicized sentence but all the rules of grammar were violated. The result is that even though all the correct words were present, the sentence cannot convey any significant meaning. Lindbeck's cultural-linguistic approach to theological doctrines functions kind of like that, which is the most one can say. It is something like a rule of grammar. The language we use about God is more like a "rule of grammar" than an exact mental description of an object or an expression of an experience that need not take into account rules of grammar at all.

Many people find this unsatisfying. Some think it says too much; some think it says too little. Analytic theologians who want theology to be more exact, more of a precise science, find that it says too little. They think theological terms can be analyzed more precisely than this kind of "obscure" linguistic approach allows. Like their counterparts in analytic philosophy, they strive for a more exact analysis of the various concepts we use in theology trying to fix their meaning more precisely. They would find this move to language and culture to be something of a retreat from a careful, logical analysis. They

2. Ibid., 18.

would privilege logic over culture. However, the cultural-linguistic approach does not deny the importance of logic, but it denies there is a single logic, universally expressible through any language or culture. This is why cultures matter. Cultures have a kind-of-logic that tends to evaporate when you fix its meaning to carefully detailed statements. This would be like the vivisection of a frog. It can be helpful in showing component features of something we call "frog," but it does so only by taking the life out of the frog. An analytical approach to theology does the same to its living language; it takes away its life.

While analytic theology finds the cultural-linguistic approach to say too little about theology, postmodern feminist theology finds Lindbeck's cultural-linguistic approach says too much for it still assumes that Christian theology has a distinct content and a distinct language. For postmodern feminist theology, the postliberals find too much "stability" in Christianity and thus have not taken the analysis of "cultures" as far as they should. Cultures are not internally, consistent wholes that provide stable identities. No such thing exists. That kind of stable identity does not exist except when some authority tries to force all differences into the strictures of a single interpretation. This assumes too much unity, and claims for unity are often disguised power plays. The theological task is never to be wedded to a past or present cultural achievement, but always to remain open to the Word of God as it comes in fresh and new modes.[3] Thus the theological task is always to deconstruct supposed stable identities of doctrine or practice in order to show how they are power plays, or illusory.

3. See Tanner, *Theories of Culture*, 49, 150, and 164.

This is quite similar to Niebuhr's call for a permanent revolution based on a radical monotheism; it is no surprise that many of the strongest proponents for this kind of theology come from a Reformed tradition. But postmodern feminist theology also argues that Christian theology is defined less by its own intrinsic content and more by its oppositional differences to others, which are always shifting. All Christian content is finally "borrowed" from materials at hand, and thus, as Kathryn Tanner puts it in her *Theories of Culture*, "One cannot sum up, for more than a particular time and place, the resemblances that tie together the Christian uses of borrowed materials, since the pattern that weaves those practices together may be constantly changing by God's free grace."[4] The Reformed emphasis on God's utter sovereignty always calls into question any cultural achievement, relativizing it to a particular time and place that may not serve the needs of the present generation.

Tanner's postmodern feminist theology is more of a "style" of theology than a distinct practice or culture. Christianity never has enough of its own substance such that it can be an "alternative society" or a distinct culture. Inasmuch as theology has to do with "style," postmodern theology is similar to another important theological movement that relates theology and culture, known as "radical orthodoxy," which will be discussed below. But if postmodern feminist theology argues Christianity in no way functions as a culture with a logic intrinsic to its own language, it differs greatly from radical orthodoxy. Thus, Kathryn Tanner, one of the ablest proponents of postmodern feminist theology, finds that radical

4. Ibid., 147.

orthodoxy, like Lindbeck's postliberal theology, assumes a too easily defined and stable Christian identity. Radical orthodox theologians would tend to find Tanner's position too allied to certain trends in postmodernity that identify cultures only by what they oppose, that is to say, these postmodern accounts of culture tend to be "reactive." Because they do not contain any inherent logic internal to their practices, they can only be identified by their adoption and opposition to the borrowed cultural products that can alone allow us to recognize them at all. This means that they are not only "mediating," which is to say that they express theology by mediating it in and through available cultural forms, but they are also "accommodating," they accommodate those cultural forms to such an extent that they finally subordinate the logic inherent in Christianity to the logic inherent in the secular rationality by which most accounts of culture are presented to us, especially as they are given to us by the social sciences.

Questions for Reflection

1. How does Lindbeck's cultural-linguistic approach qualify Tillich or Niebuhr's understanding of the relationship between theology and culture?

2. What are the strengths and limits to Lindbeck's approach?

3. What are the strengths and limits to the analytic approach?

4. Does Christianity have a stable identity over time?

5. Is there a 'logic' internal to Christian faith?

6. What is the relationship between culture and logic?

7. What makes theology mediating?

8. What makes theology accommodating?

12

Contemporary Theology II: Radical Orthodoxy, Communio Catholicism, Anabaptist Witness

Radical orthodoxy began at Cambridge University in the 1990s, primarily among Anglican theologians. Its beginning can be traced to John Milbank's *Theology and Social Theory*, which argued that modern theologians had allowed their work to be "policed" by the logic intrinsic to the secular social sciences and there was no need for this to continue to take place. He set forth a different logic in Christianity primarily based on the doctrine of the incarnation. Yet one of the most difficult aspects of this theology is defining precisely what it is.[1] It has been called more of a "sensibility" than a movement or school of theology. Like communio catholic theology, it draws heavily on the work of de Lubac and von Balthasar. It bears some similarities to Lindbeck's post-liberal theology; it assumes theology privileges the gift it receives through the

---

1. Fortunately, we now have James K. Smith's *Introducing Radical Orthodoxy*, which explains it at an introductory level and shows how it is not only from Methodists, Anglicans, and Catholics, but also can be done within the Calvinist tradition.

church's worship. As Catherine Pickstock argues, "liturgy consummates philosophy."[2] But inasmuch as post-liberal theology assumes that the theological task is simply to engage in self-description, then radical orthodoxy parts company with it. (I don't think this characterizes post-liberal theology, although some radically orthodox theologians suggest that it does.) Radical orthodoxy claims to be "more mediating" than post-liberal theologies, which means that it has more interest in relating theology to cultural institutions, to music, art, economics, politics, the university, etc. This could make it sound similar to correlational and postmodern feminist theologies, but radical orthodoxy also distances itself from them as well. It claims to be "less accommodating" to modern cultural concepts than theologies that either correlate to, or accommodate, modernity. It claims to be "orthodox" in sensibility, committed to the heritage of Christian doctrine that is the legacy of the early church and was developed up to, and even through, the modern era. Radical orthodoxy is often characterized as a "postmodern Augustinian Thomism," which means that it assumes with posmodernity that there is no neutral, objective rationality or logic that positions every other form of reasoning or logic. But it does not then abandon the idea that Christianity does have its own distinct universal logic as some postmodern feminists do. It uses the work of St. Augustine and St. Thomas Aquinas to fill the void postmodernity intentionally creates in modern culture. This is something postmodern feminism usually finds highly objectionable. But radical orthodoxy is also radical in that it uses this theological heritage to engage, critique, and supplement

2. See Pickstock, *After Writing*.

modern cultural institutions, showing how they border on nihilism. They always deconstruct every account of the good, the true, and the beautiful finding in it a disguised power play. They seek to liberate us from these power plays so that we can be free, but then the question arises, free for what? Just to be free from everything would be to be free for nothing, which is what "nihilism" means. Radical orthodoxy seeks to fill this void in modern and post-modern cultural institutions not by destroying them, but by claiming that only theology can finally preserve them. This is an ambitious claim, exactly what it means or looks like proponents of radical orthodoxy have not yet been able to show us.

Like the radically orthodox theologians, communio catholic theologians are much less worried than postmodern feminists that every claim to unity and truth is a disguised power play. They want to recover a culture and politics that can speak more easily about truth, goodness, and beauty than can modern or postmodern culture. But they also find the analytic theologians falling prey to too much of the logic of modern culture by instrumentalizing reason and treating it primarily as a search for true propositions that can be known irrespective of one's cultural context.

"Communio" Catholics take their name from an important international journal that arose out of the tradition of the *nouvelle théologie*. Unlike postmodern feminists, correlationists, and accomodationist theologies, communio theology finds modern culture to be inhospitable to Christian faith, especially Catholic faith. Communio Catholics find modern theology to be an outgrowth of Protestant culture that tempts Catholics to be "Catholic in faith" but "Protestant in culture."

Its emphasis on the individual and the voluntary nature of all modern social institutions—the nation-state founded on the "will" of the people, the market based on peoples' "preferences," the university understood as the "marketplace of ideas," the corporation grounded in maximization of profit, and even the church understood primarily as a "voluntary gathering"—run so counter to Catholic sensibilities and so thoroughly dominate the United States and much of the world that Catholics are in danger of losing their culture by being swallowed up in the modern-Protestant-American culture. Like radical orthodoxy, this position also creates great controversy at present. Many Catholic theologians worked diligently to find a place in modernity and in America for Catholicism even when both modernism and "Americanism" were condemned by Popes. They made great strides in overcoming America's suspicion of Roman Catholics for prior to the 1960s most American feared Catholics would be more loyal to the Pope than the President. They were not to be trusted with political power. Catholics successfully overcame this with the election of the first Catholic president, John F. Kennedy in the 1960s. Catholics came of age; they could contribute to America rather than remain at odds with it. After all, the motto at one of the most prestigious Roman Catholic universities in the country, the University of Notre Dame, is "For God, country, and Notre Dame." Some see the communio Catholics as a threat to these important accommodations and a return to the anti-modern sentiment of nineteenth-century Catholicism.

A concern that the Church has been swallowed up by a dominating modern theology also arises from another church tradition, one which you would expect differs as far from Roman Catholicism in distance and prestige as Rome does from Goshen, Indiana. This is what I will call the Anabaptist witness. Like the *nouvelle théologie*, the term "Anabaptist" was given to this group by its enemies. The *ana* in "Anabaptist" means "re-" in the sense of "again." Anabaptists are the rebaptizers, the people who baptize others again or a second time because they reject infant baptism and practice believers' baptism. (Since they don't think infant baptism is baptism, they would not accept that they are baptizing again.) They emerged in the sixteenth century after the Protestant Reformation through a variety of disparate movements, and have been called the "radical" reformers. James McClendon was an important Anabaptist theologian who wrote a work on theology and culture which he called *Witness*.

McClendon follows Sara Coakley in finding cultural relativism to be a "dead duck." No one can reasonably sustain such a position. He does, however, defend theology as a culture related activity which he calls "perspectivism." He describes this in the following terms:

"Persons or communities with different convictions will experience, think and speak about their worlds differently, and those differences will not necessarily be the result of mistakes or character flaws. But neither are [the differences] walls or electronic scramblers, making communication, understanding, or even persuasion among worlds impossible."[3]

What does McClendon's perspectivism mean? It can best be understood by the Anabaptist traditions' conviction that Christians should not use violence against their enemy. This

3. McClendon, *Witness*, 53.

conviction is part of the perspective that makes Anabaptists to be Anabaptists. One could not understand who they are without recognizing how this conviction is embodied in their worship, practices, and doctrines, and how it relates to a whole host of other convictions. The commitment to refuse to use violence against one's enemies only makes sense within a larger cultural network of convictions that constitute the Anabaptist perspective. For instance, if we ask the Anabaptists why do you practice nonviolence? Is it because you believe people are basically good and we should all just get along? They would say, no, we are not that silly. You can only understand our commitment to nonviolence if you share some of our other convictions such as that in Jesus Christ, and his refusal to use the sword against his enemies but to suffer the cross, we have the proper cultural presentation of what it means to be human. If you do not share our convictions about Jesus, you will most likely not share our convictions about nonviolence. This is not a "moral or character flaw" on your part; it just shows that we do not see the same world. It does not mean we do not share many visions of the world, nor that you cannot understand us, but to understand our vision fully you would need to share some of our convictions.

McClendon takes the word for "martyrdom," or "witness" as the basis for his theological vision. It provides a kind of window into the Anabaptist vision. The purpose of the Christian life is to be a living witness to the reality of Christ's life, death, resurrection, and ascension. Such a witness always entails cultural embodiment. McClendon's *Witness* develops a theology of culture around three central concerns of human culture: religion, education, and art. Each of these is an aspect of culture that is drawn into the Anabaptist perspective of witness. He defines them as follows:

1. Religion: "humanity reaching out to whatever lies beyond humanity," which is "humanity's response to the holiness and goodness and presence of God."

2. Science and Society: "that form of life in which a people acquires and extends the skills required to cope with nature and enjoys its goods."

3. Art: "the persistence of beliefs and practices across the generations, each new generation being initiated, socialized into the ways of the tribe, into the traditions represented by its art."[4]

Theology requires engagement with all these aspects of life. It begins with the cultivation of its own religious context through the community of faith. It itself is a cultural achievement that cultivates the "witness" through all the cultural means available to creation. Thus theology must branch out and help us to understand science and the arts. It does not do so by trying to rule over them from above, or forcing bad science like "creationism" on the educational system through the power of legislation or the courts. Instead it must bear witness consistent with Christ's own witness. This entails openness to wisdom from wherever it comes, even when we never forsake the center that gives the religious community itself a unique perspective, a center who is the Risen but crucified Christ. How does theology and culture relate for McClendon? "Theology is a 'science of convictions', not in

4. Ibid., 62.

the flabby subjective sense that is only the opinion of this or that party, but that it examines convictions, the deep assents constituting a people of conviction, connected (in theology's intent) to *whatever* else *there is*."[5] Theology engages the full ambit of human activity to draw it into a witness to the truth and goodness of God.

So what has theology to do with culture? Everything. Because Christians confess that the Triune God created the world in, through, and for Jesus Christ, no autonomous realm of culture can escape bearing witness at some level to or against Christ. In fact, every answer to the question "How do theology and culture relate?" will also be an answer as to who we think Jesus is. An answer to the question of theology and culture is always also an answer to Jesus' question to his disciples: "Who do you say that I am?" If we say, "You are the Christ, the Son of God," then we must also begin to address the question how theology and culture are related. This Jesus of Nazareth, a human creature, born of Mary, nurtured in a culture, now mediated historically in and through every culture that has arisen, arises, and will arise, is also no One less than God. An answer to the question how theology and culture relate depends on how we relate Christ's two natures: the human and the divine. Traditionally Christians have answered that in Jesus, the human remains human and God remains God, but now these two natures are found in one Person. The natures are not confused with each other, changed into each other, divided from each other nor contrasted according to their functions. Yet the two natures are One Person, who was born, lived, died, was risen from the

5. Ibid., 402.

dead, ascended to God the Father, and now mediates his body to the world through the presence of the Spirit by preaching, baptism, the Lord's Supper, the gathering of the church, and being present in it through its vocation to perform acts of mercy and justice in the world. In so doing, Christ draws all people and all cultures into his own life, sanctifying them and preparing them as a new creation. What is the relationship between theology and culture? No single answer can be given. The only proper answer is that it is a task, something Christians must always be engaged in by producing families, liturgy, architecture, universities, education, literature, poetry, music, friendships, economic arrangements, political associations, neighborhoods, and yes—even theology that can bear witness to God's goodness, glorify God in the world, sanctifying it for God's sake. Obviously the answer to the relationship between theology and culture is not found solely in the pages of any single book. It is found by looking around at the ordinary activities of everyday life and asking yourself, do you see the goodness of God in this? Can you show it to others that they might also see it?

Questions For Reflection

1. How might theology mediate cultural forms such as architecture, university life, education, literature, economic arrangements and political associations without accommodating cultural forms set against the faith itself?

2. What similarities and differences might be present among the radical orthodox, the communio Catholics and the Anabaptist emphasis on witness?

3. How would you define freedom? How does it differ from nihilism?

4. What is the relationship between theology and culture? What should it be? How does truth relate to this relationship?

Bibliography

Carter, Craig A. *Rethinking Christ and Culture: A Post-Christendom Perspective*. Grand Rapids: Brazos, 2007.

Coakley, Sarah. "Theology and Cultural Relativism." *Neue Zeitschrift für systematische Theologie und Religionsphilosophie* 21 (1979): 223–43.

Cone, James H. *A Black Theology of Liberation*. New York: Orbis, 1990.

———. *The Spirituals and the Blues: An Interpretation*. New York, 1992.

———. *Black Theology and Black Power*. New York: Orbis, 1997.

Davidson, Donald. *Inquiries into Truth and Interpretation*. New York: Oxford University Press, 1984.

Edwards, Paul, editor. *The Encyclopedia of Philosophy*. 8 vols. New York: Macmillan, 1967.

Ford, David, and Rachel Muers. *The Modern Theologians: An Introduction to Christian Theology since 1918*. 3rd ed. Oxford: Blackwell, 2005.

Guarino, Thomas G. *Foundations of Systematic Theology*. Theology for the Twenty-First Century. New York: T. & T. Clark, 2005.

Hauerwas, Stanley. *The State of the University: Academic Knowledges and the Knowledge of God*. Illuminations: Theory and Religion. Oxford: Blackwell, 2007.

Lafont, Cristina. *Linguistic Turn in Hermeneutic Philosophy*. Translated by José Medina. Studies in Contemporary German Social Thought. Cambridge: MIT Press, 1999.

Lindbeck, George A. *The Nature of Doctrine: Religion and Theology in a Postliberal Age*. Philadelphia: Westminster, 1984.

Long, D. Stephen. *Speaking of God: Theology, Language and Truth*. Grand Rapids: Eerdmans, forthcoming.

McClendon, James William, Jr. Vol. 3: *Witness. Systematic Theology*. Nashville: Abingdon, 2000.

Milbank, John. *Theology and Social Theory: Beyond Secular Reason*. 2nd ed. Political Profiles. Oxford: Blackwell, 2006.

————. *Being Reconciled: Ontology and Pardon.* Radical Orthodoxy Series. New York: Routledge, 2003.

Niebuhr, H. Richard. *Christ and Culture.* New York: Harper & Row, 1975.

Pickstock, Catherine. *After Writing: On the Liturgical Consummation of Philosophy.* Challenges in Contemporary Theology. London: Blackwell, 1997.

Rorty, Richard M., editor. *The Linguistic Turn: Essays in Philosophical Method.* Chicago: University of Chicago Press, 1992.

Rowland, Tracey. *Culture and the Thomist Tradition: After Vatican II.* Radical Orthodoxy Series. New York: Routledge, 2002.

Smith, James K. A. *Introducing Radical Orthodoxy: Mapping a Post-Secular Theology.* Grand Rapids: Baker Academic, 2004.

————. *Speech and Theology: Language and the Logic of Incarnation.* Radical Orthodoxy Series. New York: Routledge, 2002.

Stassen, Glenn H., D. M. Yeager, and John Howard Yoder. *Authentic Transformation: A New Vision of Christ and Culture.* Nashville: Abingdon, 1996.

Tanner, Kathryn. *Theories of Culture: A New Agenda for Theology.* Guides to Theological Inquiry. Fortress Press, 1997.

Taylor, Charles. *Philosophy and the Human Sciences.* Vol. 2, *Philosophical Papers.* Cambridge: Cambridge University Press, 1985.

Tillich, Paul. *Theology of Culture.* Edited by Robert Charles Kimball. New York: Oxford University Press, [1959] 1964.

————. *The Dynamics of Faith.* New York: Harper, 1957.

Troeltsch, Ernst. *The Social Teaching of the Christian Churches.* Translated by Olive Wyon. 2 vols. Chicago: University of Chicago Press, 1981.

Weber, Max. "Politics as a Vocation." In *From Max Weber: Essays in Sociology,* edited by H. H. Gerth and C. Wright Mills, 77–128. New York: Oxford University Press, 1946.

Williams, Raymond. *Keywords: A Vocabulary of Culture and Society.* Rev. ed. New York: Oxford University Press, 1985.

Winch, Peter. *The Idea of a Social Science and its Relation to Philosophy.* Routledge Classics. London: Routledge, 2007.

Žižek, Slavoj. *The Plague of Fantasies.* New York: Verso, 1997.